Fast, Fresh & Green

Fast, Fresh & Green

More Than 90 Delicious Recipes for Veggie Lovers

By Susie Middleton

Photographs by Ben Fink

CHRONICLE BOOKS
SAN FRANCISCO

In memory of my grandmother Honey

Library of Congress Cataloging-in-Publication Data available.

ISBN 978-0-8118-6566-1

Manufactured in China

Designed by Jessica Hische
Prop styling by Susie Middleton
Food styling by Michelli Knauer

10 9 8 7 6 5 4 3 2

Chronicle Books LLC
680 Second Street
San Francisco, California 94107
www.chroniclebooks.com

Contents

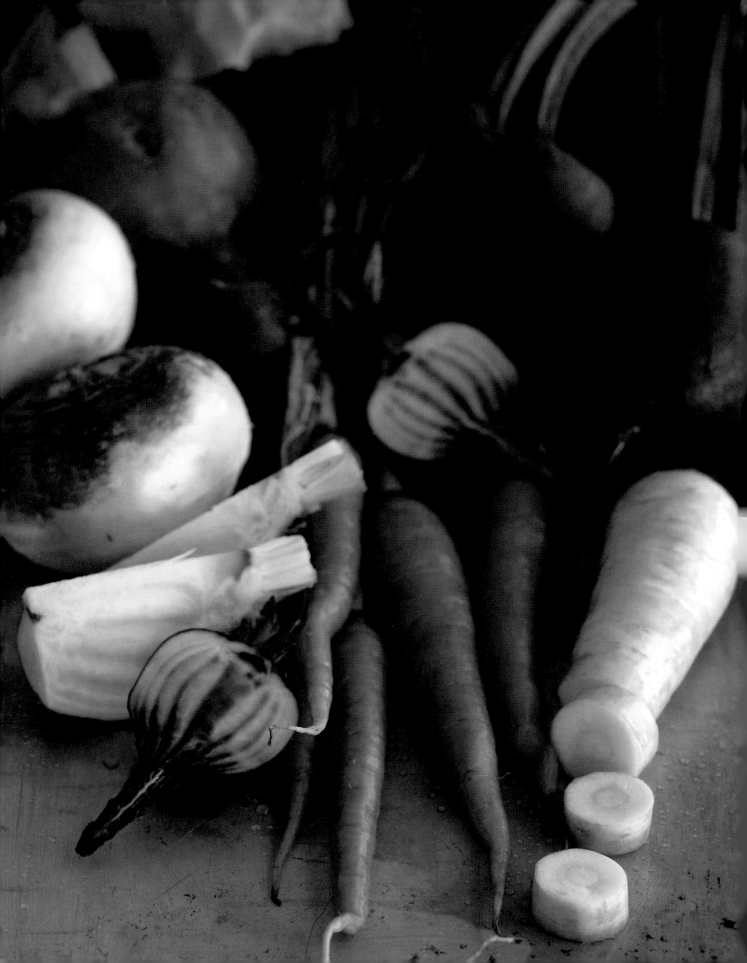

Getting into the Zone

I start thinking about dinner when I wake up in the morning. I know—I'm crazy like that. Fortunately, I usually get distracted by breakfast. Most mornings I'm busy figuring out how I can design yet another killer egg sandwich. Today I stuffed my butter-broiled English muffin with some really sharp Vermont cheddar cheese, one of my roasted tomatoes (page 41), and an egg from a farm I like to visit, scrambled up with a bit of cream and a few chives. Did I mention I like to cook? For myself, my friends, my ninety-three-year-old father-in-law, even the dog.

I'm sorry, I don't mean to be making a big deal out of it; it's just that I want you to know that this is a *cookbook*—and a highly personal one at that. It's my gift to you, because I love helping people learn to become better cooks. And I don't mean that in the "I am wearing a chef's coat and you are quivering in your clogs wondering when the fun begins" kind of way. I'm just offering up all the tips and techniques I know about cooking vegetables—and more than 90 recipes to mess around with. In my years as editor of *Fine Cooking* magazine, I got downright evangelical about vegetables—not because I'm a health nut, but because I think they taste so much better when properly cooked. And because I know everyone would like to eat more of them.

Despite the name of this book—*Fast, Fresh & Green*—I don't want you to think that it's all about speed. You *will* absolutely learn to turn out delicious vegetable side dishes—many, many of them in under 30 minutes. I promise. But you will also be chopping and stirring—*cooking*—and, well, loving it. At first, you may stumble a bit and find that some things take you a little longer than you'd like. (If that happens, just stop and make a recipe like Sautéed Sugar Snap Peas with Salami Crisps on page 85 or Brown Butter Summer Squash "Linguine" on page 93 and you will feel better. They're ultra-easy and fast.) A few (very delicious) recipes may even take 45 or 50 minutes. But once you start tasting what you've cooked—and hear the roars from your crowd—you'll feel great.

Then one day you'll find yourself coming home from work or school or a busy round of errands and automatically turning the oven on or pulling out your sauté pan—because you've already decided how you'll cook your veggies, and what you want to make with them. You might not even need to look at the recipe anymore. It might be Sautéed Carrots with Warm Olive and Mint Dressing (page 87) or Gingery Braised Brussels Sprouts (page 62). Or maybe Vanilla and Cardamom Glazed Acorn Squash (page 51). You'll be dreaming about how delicious it is going to be before you even start. You may just forget about the steak or chicken altogether.

"How is all this going to happen?" you might be asking. Well, I'm going to encourage you to make a little mind shift. I want you to think about *how* you're going to cook before you think about *what* you're going to cook. Do you feel like grilling tonight (easy on the cleanup)? Want to turn the oven on to do some roasting, which means hands-off cooking? Maybe you feel like stir-frying or sautéing to ease your tensions. Deciding which method you'll use to cook your vegetables (there are nine in this book) is the first step in a strategy I'm going to share with you for creating yummy vegetable side dishes every night. It's an approach I've developed over the years, which I think will help prevent the problem we've all had of standing in front of the refrigerator at six o'clock in the evening, staring dumbfounded at a bag of carrots.

When I get home from a long day, the first thing I do (after petting my dog, feeding my dog, letting my dog out, and, oh, petting my dog again) is turn on the oven, light my grill, or get out my sauté pan or skillet. Next I rummage through that fridge, or more precisely, the vegetable bin. I begin to look at what I've got and imagine some kind of yummy vegetable thing. (I almost always keep meats simple on weeknights—grilled skirt steak, roasted chicken thighs, seared pork tenderloin—and let my vegetable side dishes bring the interest and excitement to the plate.) If I'm lucky, there's a stash of good stuff in that vegetable bin. I buy local produce directly from the farm or the farmers' market when I can these days, and, not surprisingly, it usually lasts a lot longer than the store-bought, trucked-in, poly-bagged stuff. But like everyone else, I'm often stuck with whatever I've managed to get at the grocery store on Sunday, and it may not be the absolute freshest. (I realize that may seem like a heretical admission in a book like this, but we all have to do our best.)

Once I've pulled a few vegetables out of the fridge, I rifle through the pantry—and the fridge again—to look for flavor ideas, like hoisin sauce, fresh ginger, and a few scallions; or sherry vinegar, briny capers, lemon, and fresh parsley (see The Pantry, on page 11). Once I've got the flavors going, if I haven't already, I grab the right pan for the job—heavy-duty sheet pans for roasting, a heavy-duty straight-sided sauté pan for sautéing or braising, or a midweight stir-fry pan for stir-frying. Then I start slicing and dicing my vegetables. So my weeknight vegetable improvisation goes like this:

1. *I pick my cooking method.*
2. *I pick my vegetables.*
3. *I pick my flavorings.*
4. *I start chopping.*

I say "improvisation," because that's a word I'm comfortable with after years of developing vegetable recipes. But don't be scared by that expression, because I'm not asking you to improvise in this book (unless you want to!). What I'm really offering you is a strategy, and a wealth of recipes organized around eight simple techniques: quick-roasting, quick-braising, hands-on sautéing, walk-away sautéing, two-stepping, no cooking, stir-frying, and grilling. (As a bonus, I've included a ninth "slower-but-worth-it" chapter, Baking Gratins, for weekend vegetable cooking, because making these yummy casseroles is so satisfying.) With these techniques, you, too, can start thinking about what to cook based on what you want to turn on, how involved you want to be in the cooking, how much time you have, what flavors you're craving, and what results you're looking for. Now you've got options, no matter what you've got in the vegetable bin.

Yet I also want you to know that I'm not asking you to think *too* hard about these techniques. People have different cooking—and learning—styles. I find most people like to just dive right in and try a few recipes before necessarily putting a name to what they're doing. That's why there are recipes in each chapter that you could turn to right this minute and start making. (Though I would be really happy if you'd take a quick glance at the tips in the chapter introductions first!) But each chapter has a foundation recipe, so if you decide on a certain technique or a certain vegetable and don't have all the flavorings that a specific recipe calls for, you can take a few liberties and create your own vegetable side dish. And in the process, you'll learn a few of the fundamentals of that technique. You'll find it gets to be sort of a game—one you'll be really good at.

I just have to warn you about one other funny thing that may happen to you after you've cooked out of this book for a bit. While all of the recipes are designed to be side dishes, you might find yourself eating them as main dishes (especially some of the heartier recipes, like the quick-braises, the walk-away sautés, and, of course, the gratins). Or you might do as we do in our house and make dinner out of two or more of them, along with some good bread. So be open-minded; sometimes a side dish is a main dish in disguise.

A note to vegetarians (and the rest of you!):

While my meals tend to be vegetable-centric, I am not a vegetarian, and I did not set out to write a vegetarian book. But, as it happens, I wound up with a book that is 75 percent vegetarian recipes. Most of the other recipes can be transformed into vegetarian dishes by replacing the chicken broth with a high-quality vegetable broth diluted with some water. As much as I love pork fat, I only used pancetta, ham, or salami in about a dozen recipes. I think that's because the techniques I use and the other ingredients I include to build flavor make a meaty boost unnecessary. Aromatic vegetables such as onions and garlic, mushrooms and peppers, even the cabbage crowd, contribute a huge depth of flavor when they're allowed to brown and caramelize, helping us to make exciting vegetable dishes, which are often more enticing than the meat on the plate!

PART I: PREP

Chapter 1
The
Pantry

Get Personal—Stock up with
Your Favorite Flavors

My pantry has a distinctly Mediterranean flair, probably because the biggest influence on my cooking style was the time I spent working for George Germon and Johanne Killeen at the award-winning Al Forno restaurant in Providence, Rhode Island. Technically, I guess you could say Al Forno's cuisine is Northern Italian, but what George and Johanne are really known for is fresh, simple cooking that is also hearty and highly flavorful without being heavy or overwrought. Even when I worked at the restaurant more than fifteen years ago, almost every ingredient was brought in from local farms and purveyors on a daily basis. There was no walk-in refrigerator and only a very small chest freezer (to hold the canisters for made-to-order ice cream), so all of the raw ingredients were fresh. Both the ovens and the open grills (to cook Al Forno's famous grilled pizza) were wood-fired, and that's where I fell in love with roasting and grilling—and the intense flavor that high-heat cooking brings to so many things, especially vegetables.

When working with fresh ingredients (even ones that aren't just straight off the farm!) and good cooking techniques, you don't necessarily need an army of condiments to make things taste good. But having a pantry stocked with some carefully chosen, high-quality ingredients, will make it easier—and more fun—to create high-flavor dishes when you want to. (By "pantry" I mean not only cupboards, but the refrigerator and freezer, too.) At Al Forno, I came to appreciate the bright flavors of fresh herbs, citrus fruits, aromatics like garlic and shallots, and especially good-quality olive oils and vinegars. George and Johanne also bought the best Parmigiano-Reggiano cheese and prosciutto (dry-cured Italian ham), and used it judiciously.

While my pantry leans toward Mediterranean, it definitely reflects my French culinary training, too. One of the biggest secrets to cooking is "layering" flavors, which means that you season food at different stages of cooking. To do this well, it helps to understand how an ingredient will add a different character, depending on when it is added to the dish. (Think about what garlic does, for instance, at different stages of cooking.)

The French never miss an opportunity to maximize yumminess (that's Susie-speak, not French). One way they do this is by making a pan sauce—incorporating all the flavors that have developed in a dish in a marvelous finish. To make a pan sauce, you need some flavorful liquids (chicken broth, juice, wine, etc.) to deglaze, or wash off, the delicious browned bits that stick to the bottom of the pan. And then sometimes you need just a very small amount of fat—butter or cream—to finish the sauce and give it body. So you will find these things in my pantry. And when I'm using a technique that doesn't lend itself to making a pan sauce, I'll often flavor a dish with some other French-inspired "sauce" like a vinaigrette or a flavored butter (nothing too fancy). That's when I go to my pantry for things like Dijon mustard, honey, olives, capers, and sun-dried tomatoes.

I like Chinese, Thai, Mexican, and Indian flavors, too, so I keep a minimal pantry of seasonings from these cuisines, things like hoisin sauce and sesame oil, coconut milk and fish sauce, and spices like cumin, coriander, and ground chiles. And in my fridge I keep fresh ginger, which I love for its knock-out flavor and its versatility.

In telling you my flavor influences, I'm simply trying to convey to you that a pantry is a highly personal thing. You should have fun putting yours together. The list I've provided is the actual list of pantry ingredients I used in this book—every single one of them, unless I've overlooked something. (And I'm sorry to say, if you hate garlic, you are out of luck, because it's in a lot of recipes!)

Keep in mind that you don't have to buy everything at once. But there are some items you might not be familiar with, like crunchy pepitas (pumpkin seeds), which you will find you use again and again if you have them around. And, as a general piece of advice, the more you keep on hand, the more the word "quick" comes into play when making vegetable side dishes (no extra trips to the store).

If you are a more experienced cook, you likely have many of these ingredients already, so you should feel free to embellish this list as you please. You may find that once you get the gist of a walk-away sauté, for example, you want to try one with your own flavor combination.

For a moment, however, I'm going to ignore your experience level, and, since I'm not shy, tell you which things on this list I think are not embellishments, but essentials. Aromatic vegetables such as (you guessed it) garlic, shallots, and onions top that list. Fresh herbs like thyme, rosemary, and parsley. Lemons and limes, good extra-virgin olive oil, a decent vinegar, and kosher salt might round out the list. But I probably couldn't live without good Parmigiano-Reggiano cheese, either! Oh, and, sorry, cream and butter. (No, that's not the French influence sneaking in. It's the cooking of my grandmother Honey, who would make the best succotash out of our fresh Delaware corn and lima beans by adding nothing more than our local dairy's 43 percent fat-heavy cream and some salt and pepper.) But the fat I use most in this book is extra-virgin olive oil. For cooking, I buy a good grocery-store brand like Berio in bulk containers. I save my favorite Spanish extra-virgin, Nuñez de Prado, for finishing.

I've organized this list according to where you'd keep these items, and I hope that's helpful. Some things start out life in the cupboard and need to migrate to the fridge when they're opened. Remember, too, that spices lose their oomph after a year or so, so you'll need to keep an eye on replacing them. (And if you don't remember how long you've had that container of cumin, it's probably time to throw it out.) Now it's time to go shopping!

In the Cupboard

Condiments

Most of these condiments should be refrigerated after opening. I call exclusively for chicken broth (particularly low-sodium) in this book, because vegetable broths vary quite a bit in quality. Many of them taste like liquid celery, so I hate to recommend them. That said, I have found an occasional good one (I like the organic brand that my grocery store packages). So if you are a vegetarian and have found a broth you like, feel free to use it. Diluting the stronger-tasting ones with water helps, too.

ANCHOVIES

BLACK BEANS, *fermented Chinese*

BLACK BEAN SAUCE
(I like Lee Kum Kee brand)

BROTH, LOW-SODIUM CHICKEN, *in cartons*

CAPERS *(preferably salt-packed; rinse before using)*

CHILI-GARLIC SAUCE
(I like Huy Fong brand)

COCONUT MILK

FISH SAUCE *(I like Tiparos brand)*

HOISIN SAUCE *(I like Lee Kum Kee brand)*

HONEY, *light and dark (preferably local)*

HORSERADISH, *prepared*

HOT SAUCE, *a few kinds (I like Tabasco and the Asian hot sauce known as sriracha)*

KETCHUP

MAPLE SYRUP, *pure*

MAYONNAISE

MOLASSES

MUSTARD, DIJON

OYSTER SAUCE *(I like Lee Kum Kee brand)*

SOY SAUCE, *low-sodium and regular*

SUN-DRIED TOMATOES, *packed in oil*

TAPENADE

TOMATO PASTE

VANILLA EXTRACT

WORCESTERSHIRE SAUCE

Sugars and Dried Fruit

These items do not have to be refrigerated after opening. However, they do keep best tightly covered, either in a zip-top bag or a plastic or glass container.

APRICOTS, *dried*

CHERRIES, *dried*

CRANBERRIES, *dried*

SUGAR, DARK BROWN

SUGAR, GRANULATED

Nuts and Seeds

Once you've opened the sealed container, can, or jar, nuts keep best (and for the longest amount of time) in the freezer. Their natural oils tend to make them go rancid at room temperature. I find hazelnuts and pine nuts spoil more quickly than the rest, followed by walnuts. In addition to keeping most of my nuts in the freezer, I always keep a cup or two of my favorites, especially pecans and pine nuts, toasted and in a jar in my fridge to use at a moment's notice.

ALMONDS, *sliced and whole*  PEPITAS (*Mexican pumpkin seeds*)

CASHEWS | PINE NUTS (*a.k.a. pignoli*)

HAZELNUTS | SESAME SEEDS

PEANUTS | WALNUTS

PECANS

On the Counter

Aromatics

Store these in a bowl near your work area. Replace them when you see green shoots!

GARLIC | SHALLOTS

ONIONS, *yellow, red, and (in season) sweet*

Oil and Vinegar

For cooking, buy extra-virgin olive oil in large quantities (less expensive) and transfer it to a small bottle fitted with a bartender's speed pour. You can also fit some of your most frequently used vinegar bottles with those handy pouring spouts. Buy them at liquor stores. Keep your bottle of olive oil near your work area. Other oils and vinegars are best stored in a cool, dry cabinet.

OIL, CANOLA | VINEGAR, CIDER

OIL, EXTRA-VIRGIN OLIVE | VINEGAR, RED-WINE

OIL, PEANUT | VINEGAR, SHERRY

OIL, SESAME | VINEGAR, UNSEASONED RICE

OIL, VEGETABLE | VINEGAR, WHITE BALSAMIC

VINEGAR, BALSAMIC | VINEGAR, WHITE-WINE

In the Liquor Cabinet

Chances are, you keep three of these things on hand, anyway. But if you don't, buy small or minibottles. Remember not to cook with any wine you wouldn't drink.

RICE WINE	VODKA
SHERRY, DRY	WINE, DRY WHITE

In the Fridge

This is a big list. Obviously, you don't need to keep all of these herbs and cheeses on hand at one time. However, Parmigiano cheese is something that does keep for weeks in the fridge, so I am virtually never without it. I also usually keep fresh thyme and rosemary in my fridge (after the frost comes and I can no longer harvest my plants). These hardy herbs will keep best wrapped in damp paper towels and placed inside zip-top bags. I keep parsley, stems down, in a tall glass of water, leaves covered by a zip-top bag. This cool little greenhouse will keep it fresh for a week.

APPLE CIDER *(in season)*	HAM, *thinly sliced*
APPLES	HERBS, *fresh (basil, cilantro, mint, oregano, parsley, rosemary, sage, tarragon, thyme, and lemongrass, which you can slice and keep in the freezer)*
BUTTER, UNSALTED	
BLUE CHEESE *(good quality in a hunk, not crumbled)*	
	JUICES *(mango, orange, and pomegranate)*
CHEDDAR	LEMONS
GRUYÈRE	LIMES
FETA	OLIVES, PITTED KALAMATA
GOAT CHEESE, *fresh*	ORANGES, BLOOD
MOZZARELLA, *fresh*	ORANGES, NAVEL
PARMIGIANO-REGGIANO	PESTO
SWISS CHEESE	PROSCIUTTO
CHILES, FRESH SERRANO	SALAMI
CREAM, HEAVY	SCALLIONS
EGGS	SOUR CREAM
GINGER, *fresh*	YOGURT, WHOLE PLAIN *(preferably Greek-style)*

In the Freezer

To make fresh bread crumbs, pulse ripped-up bread (I like English muffins) in a food processor or a coffee grinder. Store in zip-top bags. Separate bacon and pancetta into smaller portions suitable for one recipe, and store the portions, wrapped in plastic, in one or two zip-top bags.

BACON	BREAD CRUMBS, *fresh*
BREAD, *sliced artisan*	PANCETTA

In the Spice Cabinet

In recipes for quick vegetable side dishes, there isn't a lot of time for spices to release their flavors, so I use them less often than fresh herbs. (Your pantry will most likely contain more spices than this suggested list.) If you're buying a spice blend, for example curry powder, make sure it's not one of the brands that has added salt, or your finished dish will wind up too salty.

CARDAMOM, *ground*	GINGER, *crystallized*
CINNAMON, *ground*	PAPRIKA, SWEET HUNGARIAN
CHILE POWDER, ANCHO	PAPRIKA, SPANISH SMOKED (*a.k.a. pimentón de la Vera*)
CHILE POWDER, CHIPOTLE	
COCOA POWDER, *unsweetened*	PEPPERCORNS, BLACK
CORIANDER, *ground*	RED PEPPER, CRUSHED (*also called flakes*)
CUMIN, *ground*	SALT, KOSHER
CURRY POWDER	SALT, COARSE SEA (*preferably fleur de sel or Maldon*)

Chapter 2
The Vegetables

From the Grocery Cart to the Fridge to the Stove—
Shopping, Storing, and Cooking Your Vegetables

Let's assume that your pantry is stocked up. Now all you need to do is go vegetable shopping, bring home your loot, and start cooking.

I'm going to offer just a few tips for shopping and storing your vegetables, but go ahead and explore your culinary options. You have a choice—you can decide what side dish to make by choosing one of the nine techniques in the following chapters, or you can utilize the index in the back of the book to choose a recipe according to the vegetable you want to cook. You will find prepping information for each vegetable in the recipes.

Shopping Like a Pro

Offering advice about shopping for vegetables always makes me feel a little silly. "Don't buy asparagus with slimy tips. Don't buy potatoes that are shrunken and dried up. Don't buy moldy cucumbers." Hello! We all know not to buy rotten produce; that's obvious. What's not so clear sometimes is which vegetables are of the best quality, which ones will taste great, and, yes, which ones are about to go bad (but aren't yet in full demise).

I thought about this for a bit, thought about how I've absorbed this information over the years, and I realized there's just one secret to choosing vegetables: practice. Become a frequent vegetable shopper. By that I don't mean shopping every day of the week. I mean, if you want to get friendly with, say, eggplant, buy it several weeks in a row in the summer, when it's in season. Buy some at the farmers' market, get one from your neighbor's garden, and buy some at the grocery store. Buy a few big globe eggplants, a few slim Japanese ones, and a couple of small white ones. Grill some, roast some, sauté some. Suddenly by Labor Day, you're an eggplant expert. Better than reading anything I can tell you about how an eggplant's skin should give ever so slightly when it's perfectly ripe is the experience you'll have of cutting into a few young ones with very taut skin and finding them a bit green inside (or, at the opposite extreme, picking up one that's been in the fridge for too long and finding that your hand leaves deep fingerprints in it).

If you follow my suggestion and buy vegetables from different places (and even from different suppliers in the same market), you'll begin to learn what sources to trust. And you'll begin to understand why people like me jump up and down and beg you to buy the freshest vegetables possible (preferably ones that are in season locally and not shipped many thousands of fuel-saturated miles to get to you). You will be amazed at how much longer the vegetables you buy at a farmers' market (or dig from your own garden) last than those you bring home from the Super Star Deluxe Big Box Grocery.

And, yes, you will be amazed at how much better locally grown vegetables taste. Get in the habit of tasting your vegetables raw (if you can) before cooking with them. You'll begin to notice subtle—and sometimes not-so-subtle—differences. Compare a young carrot that has been harvested locally (and hopefully grown in organic soil) to an older one that has been shipped from afar and conventionally raised in soil that is most likely nutrient-depleted. I picked those carrots because they're such a good example of the range of sweetness to bitterness that a vegetable can have. (And those older carrots, even with the magic of roasting or sautéing, will still unfortunately, retain some bitterness.) You can do this kind of taste comparison with other vegetables. For example, once you taste the distinctly nutty and spicy flavor of an arugula leaf from a fresh, loose, bunch, you might be more willing to wash the sand off it, rather than put up with the lackluster flavor of arugula leaves packed in a plastic bag or box, which was shipped days or weeks ago.

A few last things to think about when you're at the grocery store: In general, buy vegetables that have been processed or packaged as little as possible. For instance, don't buy sliced mushrooms or shredded cabbage if you can help it. Once cut, these veggies are going to spoil much more quickly. Look at labels and see where produce is coming from. Since I live on the East Coast, if I can't buy local produce, I will buy whatever is in or closest to this region. I buy New Jersey blueberries, New York apples, and Maine potatoes when they're available. I also keep my eyes out for variety labels, which are more common now. In the sweet potato bin, for example, there may be a mix of Jewels and Garnets and Gems (all lovely!), and it is fun to try different ones to see what you like. Unfortunately, there is still a lot of mislabeling and confusing labeling in the grocery store, too, so don't be afraid to ask someone if you're not sure whether you've got bok choy or Napa cabbage in your hands.

Smart Storage

I love the idea of shopping on a Sunday afternoon, because you can come home and do some prep for the week. With a few extra minutes, you can wash, store, and, in some cases, even precook vegetables, saving time later on a weeknight. But even if you aren't a Sunday afternoon shopper, these are all smart ideas for keeping your veggies in good shape through the week.

Leafy Greens or Lettuce

Stem, wash, spin dry, and store loosely in zip-top bags lined with paper towels to absorb excess moisture.

Hearty Greens

Cabbage and bok choy don't discolor when cut, so go ahead and cut them before storing.

Herbs

Wrap hardy herbs, such as rosemary, in damp paper towels and store in zip-top bags. Store parsley, stems down, in a glass of water. Cover the leaves with a zip-top bag. Keep basil unrefrigerated, in a glass of water, if you bought it in a bunch or picked it yourself. If you don't plan to use it soon, wrap it carefully in damp paper towels, covering all surfaces, and store in a zip-top bag in the refrigerator. Store cilantro and mint this way, too, to prevent the oxidation of leaves. (If you bought any of these in a plastic box in a refrigerator case, though, keep it that way.)

Vegetables

Asparagus

Store stems down, in a glass of water.

Avocados

Put in brown paper bags to ripen.

Corn

When it's in season, boil ears ahead of time, slice off the kernels (see page 67), and keep them in a covered container in the fridge or freezer to be added to salads, sautés, and side dishes.

Potatoes

Put in a paper bag or a dark place (or cover with a dish towel) so that they do not turn green. Store separately from onions. Do not refrigerate.

Tomatoes

Always store at room temperature, never in the fridge; cold kills their flavor. If you have spare time, make the Caramelized Plum Tomatoes in an Olive Oil Bath (page 41). They store well and make excellent ingredients for salads and pastas later in the week.

When You're Ready to Cook

Most recipes can be cooked in about 30 minutes or less, and a dozen or so can be done in about 20 minutes. You can pretty much assume that all of the other recipes, except for those in the Baking Gratins chapter, can be done in about 45 minutes. (For any recipe that I've thought will take you longer, I've indicated the extra time needed in its headnote.) Many recipes, like those in the Quick-Roasting chapter, have a significant amount of hands-off cooking time, too. If you're short on time, you can often skip a garnish of chopped parsley or toasted nuts (especially if you're not keeping these on hand in the fridge) to speed things up. Estimated times do not include preheating the oven.

You will notice that a majority of these recipes serve three or four people, or else four or five. It's not because I like odd numbers, but rather because that's the yield of the suggested pot or pan (which are the sizes you are most likely to have and that will work best on home stoves). Of course, some recipes serve six or more. These tend to be salads and gratins, which come together in larger cooking vessels. Many recipes yield enough for two main dish servings, for a change of pace. And lots of recipes are easily doubled. To double those in the Quick-Roasting chapter, for instance, simply use two sheet pans and shift their positions halfway through cooking.

The cooking times and cuts for a vegetable are included in the recipe. Not all vegetables work in all foundation recipes. Some vegetables naturally lend themselves to certain methods, while others (like those darn carrots) seem to work with every method. All of the "workhorse" vegetables (such as broccoli, green beans, spinach, potatoes) will work in at least one of the foundation recipes, and usually more than that.

PART II: COOK

Chapter 3

Quick-Roasting

METHOD: Quick-roasting

EQUIPMENT: Large (18-x-13-x-1-in/45.5-x-33-x-2.5-cm) heavy-duty rimmed sheet pan lined with parchment paper, tongs, oven thermometer

HEAT: The oven, HOT! 450 to 475°F/230 to 245°C (Gas Mark 8 to 9)

....

Quick-Roasting: How It Works

Roast it, and they will eat it. It's just a given. If you're on a mission, like I am, to help people fall in love with vegetables, roasting is the way to do it. By now, you probably know this, and you've probably got a recipe for roasted potatoes that you turn to a few nights a week (if truth be told). What you might not know, though, is how delicious roasted broccoli and roasted cauliflower are—or that you can use a basic technique and formula to roast whatever you've got on hand, any night of the week.

To get that delicious caramelized, roasty-toasty flavor, you need just three things: a heavy-duty aluminum sheet pan, parchment paper, and a hot oven. Oh, and a sharp knife to cut your veggies and a sturdy pair of tongs to toss them wouldn't hurt.

Honestly, I know it's a drag when people say, "Buy this and buy that." But these restaurant-style sheet pans are much easier to handle than flimsy cookie sheets, they won't warp, and, most important, they'll cook your vegetables much more evenly—especially at high heat—than anything else. (Do not be tempted to use nonstick sheet pans; their dark surface will brown the vegetables before they are tender inside.) Plus, size matters; these pans are big enough (18 x 3 x 1 in./45.5 x 33 x 2.5 cm) to accommodate a pound of vegetables while giving them enough breathing room. Your vegetables will tend to steam, not brown, if they're crammed on a smaller sheet.

It's also totally worth your while to get friendly with parchment paper. (No more sticking—I will say nothing else.) This isn't too hard, considering you can order 100 premeasured sheets in a handy tube from the King Arthur Flour Web site or catalog.

I know I'm starting to sound like a QVC commercial, but I have to ask you to buy one more thing if you aspire to be the roasting queen (or king, or just hometown hero): an oven thermometer. These roasting recipes all call for cooking at pretty high temps—450 to 475°F/230 to 245°C (Gas Mark 8 to 9). If your oven is off (and most are), you might incinerate your veggies—or have to wait around for them to cook. With the help of an oven thermometer, you'll know whether your oven is running hot or cool, and you can compensate by just raising or lowering the temperature. You should feel free to use your oven's convection function for roasting vegetables; I think it makes especially crispy potatoes. You'll have to compensate by lowering your oven temperature by twenty-five degrees and checking for doneness a few minutes earlier.

There is one more secret to quick-roasting: Cut your vegetables quite thinly, or into small pieces, and they will cook quickly. (No big chunks, please.) This is how, for instance, you can actually roast beets on a weeknight. Whole beets or even quartered beets take 1 or 2 hours to cook; beets sliced thinly roast in about 20 minutes. Don't worry if your knife skills aren't perfect. Try to keep your pieces about the same size, but we're not giving out prizes for good looks.

That's it. You now have a choice. You can follow one of the recipes in this chapter, each with its own flavor twist, or you can improvise your own roasted vegetables following the foundation recipe I've provided on page 28 and the table of cooking times for vegetables, below. Be generous with oil and salt at first, then adjust for your own preferences. Flip the veggies if you like; forget about it if it bugs you. One side of your vegetables will be browner than the other if you don't flip, but they'll cook through either way.

VEGETABLES FOR ROASTING

VEGETABLE	WAY TO CUT	COOKING TIME
Acorn or delicata squash	halved, seeded, ends trimmed, ½-in/1.25-cm slices	18 to 24 minutes
Asparagus	ends trimmed	10 to 14 minutes
Beets	unpeeled ³⁄₁₆-in/5-mm slices	16 to 18 minutes
Broccoli crowns	1½-in-/3.75-cm-long florets, halved, each piece with one flat side	14 to 18 minutes
Brussels sprouts	halved	15 to 18 minutes
Butternut squash	peeled, halved, seeded, ¾-in/2-cm dice	25 to 30 minutes
Carrots	halved, ⅜-in/9.5-mm half-moon slices	18 to 20 minutes
Cauliflower	1½-in-/3.75-cm-long florets, halved, each piece with one flat side	20 to 25 minutes
Celery root	peeled, ½-in/1.25-cm dice	15 to 17 minutes
Cremini (baby bella) mushrooms	halved	25 to 30 minutes
Eggplant	¾-in/2-cm dice	25 to 30 minutes
Green beans	ends trimmed	15 to 20 minutes
Parsnips	peeled, ⅜-in/9.5-mm slices or ½-in/1.25-cm dice	16 to 20 minutes
Red or gold potatoes	⅜-in/9.5-mm slices	20 to 25 minutes
Sweet potatoes	⅜-in/9.5-mm slices or ¾-in/2-cm dice	20 to 25 minutes
Turnips	unpeeled, ⅜-in/9.5-mm slices or ½-in/1.25-cm dice	25 to 30 minutes
Zucchini	⅜-in/9.5-mm slices or ½-in/1.25-cm dice	18 to 20 minutes

Foundation Recipe for Quick-Roasting

Here's an opportunity to roast whatever you've got in the fridge or pantry tonight. If you want to roast more than one kind of vegetable on the same sheet pan, just be sure the vegetables are cut similarly and cook in about the same amount of time (see the table on page 27). And be sure you still have about 1 lb/455 g (after trimming) on a large baking sheet. Much more, and the veggies won't cook evenly or very quickly. Much less, and the veggies will tend to cook too quickly, browning too much before becoming tender and leaving the parchment paper scorched.

Three tablespoons of olive oil is a good amount for most of the vegetables; you can bring that down to two if you like, especially with a moister vegetable. Two is plenty, for example, for quick-roasting zucchini. But you might even want to go up to four tablespoons (¼ cup/60 ml) for a vegetable that can dry out or that you want super-crisp, like potatoes or sweet potatoes. Vegetables tend to be browner on the outside and moister on the inside when tossed in plenty of oil. Whatever you do, remember the smaller or the thinner you cut the vegetable, the faster it will cook. I hope you'll get a chance to use this foundation recipe for many nights of roasted vegetables, so you'll be able to figure out what you like best.

Over the years, I've moved away from mixing fresh herbs with vegetables before roasting because the herbs have a tendency to burn. I prefer to add them afterward. Here, I've included a nifty way to do that—a flavored butter that you can customize, depending on what you have on hand. And you could also pilfer a sauce or a seasoning from any of the other recipes in this chapter. The truth is, roasted vegetables can be plenty tasty with no embellishment; that's why everyone loves them.

1¼ TO 1½ LB/570 TO 680 G YOUR CHOICE OF VEGETABLE
(1 lb/455 g trimmed; see the table on page 27 for choices and how to cut them)

3 TBSP EXTRA-VIRGIN OLIVE OIL

¾ TSP KOSHER SALT

1 RECIPE FLAVORED BUTTER
(optional; recipe follows)

1.   *Preheat the oven* to 475°F/245°C (Gas Mark 9). Line a large (18-x-13-x-1-in/ 45.5-x-33-x-2.5-cm) heavy duty rimmed sheet pan with a piece of parchment paper.

2.   *Put the vegetables* in a medium mixing bowl, add the oil and salt, and toss well.

3.   *Arrange them in one layer* on the sheet pan and roast, flipping once or twice if you like, until the vegetables are tender and golden brown, between 15 and 35 minutes, depending on the vegetable. Don't worry if the parchment paper becomes quite dark.

4.   *Let the vegetables cool* for a minute or two on the sheet pan and then transfer them to a mixing bowl. Add 2 to 4 tsp of the flavored butter (if using), toss gently until it's melted, and serve.

Serves 3 or 4

FLAVORED BUTTER

This recipe is like a foundation recipe for flavored butters, which are not only infinitely variable, but also incredibly versatile. (They can be made a few days ahead, too.) Here I start with a formula something like this: For every 2 Tbsp of unsalted butter, use ½ tsp zest, ½ to 1½ tsp chopped fresh herbs, and ⅛ tsp kosher salt. The next addition can be 1 tsp of honey or maple syrup. From there, if you like big flavor, you can add a little more zest, or add a dried spice in addition to the fresh herb (for example, an orange, mint, and curry butter). If you want a bit more sweetness, add another 1 tsp honey.

These are easy and fast; microwave the butter for a few seconds to soften it before mixing. You might not use all of this on your vegetables the first night; save it and use the rest another night on roasted, grilled, or two-step vegetables. Or top a grilled steak, pork chop, or chicken breast with it. Try it on grilled bread, too.

2 TBSP UNSALTED BUTTER, *softened*

½ TSP GRATED CITRUS ZEST *(lemon, lime, or orange)*

CHOPPED FRESH HERBS, *such as 1½ tsp finely chopped fresh parsley, mint, cilantro, or basil; or 1 tsp finely chopped fresh thyme; or ½ tsp finely chopped fresh rosemary*

⅛ TSP KOSHER SALT

1 TO 2 TSP HONEY OR MAPLE SYRUP *(optional)*

½ TSP GROUND DRIED SPICE, *such as curry powder, chile powder (including chipotle), cumin, coriander, or smoked paprika*

1.   *Combine all of the ingredients* in a small bowl and mix well with a rubber spatula.

Yields 2 to 2½ Tbsp

Quick-Roasted Cauliflower with Zesty Orange-Olive Dressing

When I cooked in a busy take-out market, I used to make roasted vegetables every day. And every day, one of the market's owners would come through the kitchen and pick the roasted cauliflower out of the pans I had cooling on the counter. She loved it, and I do, too. It's so sweet that it almost tastes like candy. So don't feel timid about serving the florets hot out of the oven, unadorned. But if you want to zip them up—and make them look a little more colorful—the orange, black olive, and parsley dressing here is delicious.

Serve this dish alongside sautéed boneless pork chops with a pan sauce made from a little red wine reduction and dried fruit.

1 LB/455 G CAULIFLOWER FLORETS, *each about 1½ in/3.75 cm long with one flat side (from 1 very small head)*

3 TBSP EXTRA-VIRGIN OLIVE OIL

¾ TSP KOSHER SALT

Orange-Olive Dressing

1 TBSP EXTRA-VIRGIN OLIVE OIL

1 LARGE GARLIC CLOVE, *smashed and peeled*

2 BIG PINCHES OF CRUSHED RED PEPPER

1 TSP FINELY GRATED ORANGE ZEST

1 TBSP FINELY CHOPPED PITTED KALAMATA OLIVES (*about 3 olives*)

2 TBSP FRESH ORANGE JUICE

1 TSP RED-WINE VINEGAR

⅛ TSP SUGAR

⅛ TSP KOSHER SALT

FRESHLY GROUND BLACK PEPPER

2 TBSP CHOPPED FRESH PARSLEY

1   *Preheat the oven* to 475°F/245°C (Gas Mark 9). Line a large (18-x-13-x-1-in/45.5-x-33-x-2.5-cm) heavy-duty rimmed sheet pan with a piece of parchment paper. In a large mixing bowl, toss the cauliflower thoroughly with the olive oil and salt. Spread the florets out on the sheet pan in one layer, flat side down. Scrape out any salt and oil remaining in the mixing bowl over the cauliflower. Roast until the bottoms are browned and the tops and edges are starting to brown, 20 to 22 minutes. Remove from the oven and let cool for a few minutes.

2   *Meanwhile, make the Orange-Olive Dressing:* In a small saucepan, heat the olive oil and the garlic over medium-low heat. Simmer until the garlic is very fragrant, but not browned, 4 to 5 minutes. Remove the garlic with a slotted spoon and add the red pepper flakes, orange zest, and olives. Stir well and remove the pan from the heat. Add the orange juice, vinegar, sugar, salt, a few grinds of pepper, and the parsley. Stir well.

3   *Using tongs,* transfer the roasted cauliflower to a medium mixing bowl. Pour the dressing over the cauliflower, scraping all of it out of the saucepan, and mix thoroughly but gently. Transfer to a serving dish. Serve warm or at room temperature.

Serves 3

Roasted Broccoli Florets
with Two Dipping Sauces

Crispy broccoli florets are just dying to be finger food, as far as I'm concerned. Offer garlic butter for dipping, and who isn't going to eat their broccoli? I've included a much lighter sauce here, too, similar to a tangy Japanese ponzu, so there's something for everyone. Even if it's a weeknight, put the broccoli out on a platter, with the two sauces in little bowls nearby. You could even sauté or roast some shrimp, double the sauce amounts, and you'd have an entirely "dippable" dinner! These florets would also be fun with other finger food like spare ribs or chicken wings.

Broccoli florets roast pretty quickly. Once they get crispy, they can start to become overcooked and dry out, so check them at the early end of the cooking time. This is such an easy recipe that you can make it often and decide for yourself what degree of doneness you like.

1 LB/455 G BROCCOLI FLORETS,
*each 2 in/5 cm long with one flat side
(from 2 bunches or 4 crowns)*

3 TBSP EXTRA-VIRGIN OLIVE OIL

1 TSP KOSHER SALT

1 RECIPE GARLIC BUTTER *(page 34)*

1 RECIPE JAPANESE DIPPING SAUCE
(page 34)

1   *Preheat the oven* to 475°F/245°C (Gas Mark 9). Line a large (18- x 13 x 1 in/45.5 x 33-x-2.5-cm) heavy-duty rimmed sheet pan with a piece of parchment paper. In a large mixing bowl, toss the broccoli florets with the olive oil and salt. Spread out the broccoli, cut side down, in one layer on the sheet pan. Roast until the bottoms are browned in spots and the florets are dark and crispy around the edges, 14 to 18 minutes (the stems will still look green).

2   *Transfer the florets* to a serving platter. Put the garlic butter in a heat-proof ramekin or bowl, and put the Japanese dipping sauce in another small bowl. Serve family-style.

Serves 4

GARLIC BUTTER

This recipe yields enough for about half a recipe of the Roasted Broccoli Florets with Two Dipping Sauces. If you don't plan to make the Japanese Dipping Sauce with the broccoli, you'll want to double this one. To add a little zip to it, toss in a dash of Tabasco or some grated lemon or lime zest.

3 TBSP UNSALTED BUTTER PINCH OF KOSHER SALT

2 TSP FINELY CHOPPED FRESH GARLIC

1   *In a small skillet,* melt the butter over low to medium-low heat. Add the garlic and salt and cook, stirring, until it is soft and fragrant, about 1 minute (don't let it burn). Remove the pan from the heat. If necessary, rewarm before transferring to a ramekin or other heat-proof dipping bowl to serve.

Yields ¼ cup/60 ml

JAPANESE DIPPING SAUCE

My friend Jessica clued me in to an easy way to make your own ponzu, which is a tangy, citrusy, soy-based Japanese sauce. Simply combine soy sauce and lemon juice and dress that up a bit with grated ginger, honey, orange juice, and sliced scallions. If you like a very tangy sauce, you can skip the honey. Either way, this makes a good foil for the earthiness of roasted broccoli (or cauliflower, if you prefer). I like to put the sauce in a little glass bowl for dipping.

2 TBSP SOY SAUCE   1 TBSP FINELY CHOPPED SCALLIONS
(white parts and some light green)

2 TBSP FRESH LEMON JUICE

½ TSP GRATED FRESH GINGER

1 TBSP ORANGE JUICE

1½ TSP HONEY

1   *Combine the soy sauce,* lemon juice, orange juice, and honey in a small bowl and whisk until the honey is dissolved. Add the scallions and ginger and stir well. Transfer to a dipping bowl to serve.

Yields ¼ cup/60 ml plus 1 Tbsp

Quick-Roasted Beet Slices

I love to surprise people with these because nobody thinks that beets can be quick. For that matter, a lot of people don't even realize that they like beets until they taste these addictive "chips." They cook in less than 20 minutes, and they're delicious right off the pan, in a marinade, in a salad (page 36), or even stuffed with a bit of seasoned goat cheese to make little sandwiches. And they're good in summer or winter, warm or at room temperature. So you could consider them an equally appropriate side dish for things as diverse as roast lamb and grilled shrimp.

Exercise a bit of caution when slicing—use a very sharp knife and, if you need to, cut a little off the bottom of the beet to steady it before slicing. You're not aiming for paper-thin (those slices would burn in a 475°F/245°C oven), so you don't need a mandoline. You'll find you'll be able to cut a neat slice that's between ⅛ and ³⁄₁₆ in/ 3.25 and 5 mm if you exert steady pressure on your knife. Try to maintain a consistent thickness when slicing so that the beets will cook at close to the same rate. You can easily double this recipe using two sheet pans.

8 TO 10 OZ/225 TO 280 G BEETS *(4 or 5 small or 3 medium), trimmed, scrubbed (but not peeled), and very thinly sliced crosswise (see tip)*	**1 TBSP EXTRA-VIRGIN OLIVE OIL** **½ TSP COARSELY CHOPPED FRESH THYME** **½ TSP KOSHER SALT**

1 *Preheat the oven* to 475°F/245°C (Gas Mark 9). Line a large (18-x-13-x-1-in/45.5-x-33-x-2.5-cm) heavy-duty rimmed sheet pan with a piece of parchment paper.

2 *Put the beet slices* in a mixing bowl and toss thoroughly with the olive oil, thyme, and salt. Arrange the slices, evenly spaced, on the sheet pan (it's okay if they touch).

3 *Roast until the beets are tender,* shrunken, wrinkled, and glistening, 16 to 18 minutes. The smallest slices will be black around the edges. Let cool for a few minutes before serving or using in another recipe.

Serves 2

Tip: Put a folded piece of parchment paper or brown paper on your cutting board before slicing the beets; it will prevent your cutting board from getting stained.

Roasted Beet, Orange, and Mâche Salad with Goat Cheese and Toasted Walnuts

This pretty salad is a perfect starter for a Valentine's Day menu—as long as your honey likes beets! The sweet and earthy flavors of the oranges and beets along with the nutty flavor and delicate texture of mâche make a classic combination. If you can't find mâche, try a combination of arugula and frisée. You can also serve the dressed beets alone. To toast the nuts, see tip below.

1 RECIPE QUICK-ROASTED BEET SLICES (*page 35*)

2 TBSP ORANGE JUICE

½ TSP FINELY GRATED LEMON ZEST

½ TSP COARSELY CHOPPED FRESH THYME

½ TSP BALSAMIC VINEGAR

½ TSP MINCED FRESH GARLIC

KOSHER SALT

1 TBSP EXTRA-VIRGIN OLIVE OIL

3 CUPS MÂCHE

1 NAVEL ORANGE, *peeled, cut into quarters, and then crosswise into ½-in-/1.25-cm-thick slices*

2 OZ/60 G FIRM FRESH GOAT CHEESE

⅓ CUP/35 G COARSELY CHOPPED TOASTED WALNUTS

1   *Arrange four salad plates* on your counter. Combine the orange juice, lemon zest, thyme, vinegar, garlic, and a pinch of salt in a bowl and stir well. Transfer 2 tsp of the dressing to a small bowl. Add the olive oil and a pinch of salt to the 2 tsp of dressing and whisk. Combine the roasted beets with the remaining dressing. Toss the mâche with the olive oil mixture.

2   *Lightly scoop one-quarter of the mâche* with your hands and put it on a salad plate (at the top of the plate, around twelve o'clock). Arrange one-quarter of the orange slices and one-quarter of the beet slices (leaving the marinade behind in the bowl) on the rest of the plate. Repeat with the remaining three plates. Sprinkle a little salt over each salad. Crumble the goat cheese and sprinkle evenly over all four salads, and then do the same with the walnuts. Serve right away.

Serves 4

Tip: **To toast nuts, preheat the oven to 350°F/175°C (Gas Mark 4), spread the nuts out on a heavy-duty rimmed baking sheet, and bake until they turn a deep golden brown. They will begin to smell very fragrant when they are almost done (between 5 and 10 minutes). Keep an eye on them as they will be bitter if too dark. Let cool on the sheet; they will crisp up as they cool. Be aware that pepitas (pumpkin seeds) will puff up and begin to pop in the oven as they toast.**

Sweet Potato "Mini-Fries" with Limey Dipping Sauce and Spiced Salt

At our house, we eat these fries right off the baking sheet, doused with a little extra salt (or a little Spiced Salt; see below). They rarely make it to the table, but if they do, they look awfully cute served in individual ramekins. Sometimes we double the recipe (easily done with two sheet pans) and plop the hot pans in front of guests who are sniffing around the kitchen before dinner. We put out a little bowl of the easiest dipping sauce ever and they disappear. One thing you should know: sweet potato oven fries, though they're addictive and delicious, do not get crispy. They will get crisp around the edges, but they stay moist in the middle. (That's part of their charm; I assure you, you will still love them.)

The sauce is my quick version of the French sauce called *aïoli*, which is a garlicky mayonnaise usually spiked with lemon. I use good-quality store-bought mayonnaise, lime zest, and lime juice for a fast, sassy sauce that's just as good on grilled fish or chicken as it is on sweet potato fries.

1 LB/455 G UNPEELED SWEET POTATOES *(about 2 small)*

¼ CUP/60 ML EXTRA-VIRGIN OLIVE OIL

1 TSP KOSHER SALT, *and more for seasoning*

Limey Dipping Sauce

⅓ CUP/65 G MAYONNAISE

½ TSP FINELY GRATED LIME ZEST

1 TBSP FRESH LIME JUICE

½ TSP MINCED FRESH GARLIC

PINCH OF KOSHER SALT

Spiced Salt (optional)

1 TSP KOSHER SALT

½ TSP SUGAR

¼ TSP GROUND CINNAMON

¼ TSP GROUND CUMIN

¼ TSP GROUND CORIANDER

¼ TSP PAPRIKA

{ Continued }

1   *Preheat the oven* to 475°F/245°C (Gas Mark 9). Line a large (18-x-13-x-1-in/45.5-x-33-x-2.5-cm) heavy-duty rimmed sheet pan with a piece of parchment paper.

2   *Cut the sweet potatoes* crosswise on a slight diagonal into ⅜-in-/9.5-mm-thick slices. (If the sweet potato is very narrow at one end, you can cut slices at a very sharp angle at that end.) Cut each slice lengthwise into sticks between ¼ and ⅜ in/6.5 and 9.5 mm wide. (They will only be about 2 in/5 cm long.) Put the sticks in a mixing bowl and combine thoroughly with the olive oil and 1 tsp salt. Spread the sweet potatoes out in one layer on the baking sheet, making sure to scrape all the oil and salt from the bowl onto them.

3   *Roast for 20 minutes.* Using a spatula, flip the sticks over and continue cooking, flipping once or twice more, until the fries are nicely browned (some in spots, some all over), about 10 minutes more.

4   *To make the Limey Dipping Sauce,* combine all the ingredients in a small bowl, whisking well to blend. Let sit for 10 to 15 minutes to let the flavors marry.

5   *To make the Spiced Salt,* stir the salt and all the spices together in a small bowl.

6   *Sprinkle* some of the spiced salt or more kosher salt on the fries (be generous and do not skip this step!), toss well, and serve with the dipping sauce.

Serves 3 to 4

Roasted Green Beans and Cremini Mushrooms with Rosemary-Garlic Oil

It probably never occurred to you to roast green beans; after all, doesn't roasting turn their lovely color a drab army green? Well, brightly colored they're not; delicious they are. Wrinkly, but toasty. And with the concentrated flavor of roasted mushrooms—not to mention a little garlic and rosemary—you've got a hit. Green beans roast a little more quickly than mushrooms, so if you like, you can remove them a few minutes ahead of the mushrooms, but I think it's easiest to keep them in. If you like things quite spicy, you can add a few more red pepper flakes to the garlic and rosemary "oil" (it's really more like a paste). You could also use that flavor trio on any roasted vegetable.

This is definitely a go-to dish for sidling up to a crispy-skinned roast chicken. But it could also complement a wintery fish preparation like roasted salmon or cod baked with tomatoes, olives, and herbs.

10 OZ/285 G CREMINI *(baby bella)* MUSHROOMS, *quartered if large, halved if small*

¼ CUP/60ML PLUS 1 TSP EXTRA-VIRGIN OLIVE OIL

1 TSP KOSHER SALT

12 OZ/340 G GREEN BEANS, TRIMMED

1 TSP MINCED FRESH GARLIC

1 TSP CHOPPED FRESH ROSEMARY

⅛ TSP CRUSHED RED PEPPER FLAKES

1 Preheat the oven to 475°F/245°C (Gas Mark 9). Line a large (18-x-13-x-1-in/45.5-x-33-x-2.5-cm) heavy-duty rimmed sheet pan with a piece of parchment paper.

2 In a mixing bowl, toss the mushrooms thoroughly with 2 Tbsp of the oil and ½ tsp of the salt. Spread out the mushrooms in one layer, cut side down, on one end of the sheet pan. (They can be close together.) Toss the green beans with 1 Tbsp of the olive oil and the remaining ½ tsp of salt. Spread the green beans out in one layer on the rest of the pan. Roast until the green beans are shrunken and very wrinkled (they will be browned in spots) and the mushrooms are tender, shrunken, and beginning to brown, about 25 minutes.

3 Meanwhile, put the remaining 1 Tbsp plus 1 tsp of olive oil in a small nonstick skillet along with the garlic, rosemary, and red pepper flakes. Bring to a simmer over medium-low heat. Once the oil starts bubbling, cook for 1 minute to infuse the oil with the flavors (the rosemary will lose its color) and to soften the garlic. Remove the skillet from the heat and let sit while the vegetables finish cooking.

4 Transfer the cooked vegetables to a mixing bowl. Scrape the seasoned oil out of the skillet and over the vegetables; toss thoroughly. Transfer to a serving platter or dinner plates.

Serves 3 to 4

Caramelized Plum Tomatoes
in an Olive Oil Bath

I love these tomatoes. They couldn't be simpler to prepare, and they cook just quickly enough to deliver slow-roasted flavor on a weeknight. (They're best after 30 to 40 minutes in the oven, but if you're in a rush, they're good after 20 to 25 minutes, too.) I'm always amazed at how a hot oven turns even the most pathetic, pale plum tomatoes into deeply flavored beauties.

The generous amount of olive oil in this recipe has a purpose — as the water in the tomatoes evaporates, the oil replaces it and gently simmers and preserves the tomato flesh. When the tomatoes are finished cooking, you can lift one end and a good bit of the oil will spill out. Don't be alarmed if the edges of some of your tomatoes (or some of the juices in the pan) look a little blackened. They will still taste delicious.

These tomatoes aren't just a great side dish; they also make perfect crostini toppers, salad ingredients or even hors d'oeuvres (see page 42).

10 PLUM TOMATOES	**2 TSP FRESH THYME LEAVES** (*4 to 6 sprigs*)
½ CUP/120 ML EXTRA-VIRGIN OLIVE OIL	**BALSAMIC VINEGAR**
KOSHER SALT	**2 LARGE GARLIC CLOVES,** *peeled and sliced crosswise into 10 to 12 slices each*
SUGAR	

1 *Preheat the oven* to 425°F/220°C (Gas Mark 7). Line a large (18-x-13-x-1 in/45.5-x-33-x-2.5-cm) heavy-duty rimmed sheet pan with a piece of parchment paper. Cut each tomato in half lengthwise, and, leaving in the core, scrape out the seeds and ribs with a tomato shark or a serrated spoon. Brush 1 Tbsp of the olive oil over the parchment. Arrange the tomato halves, cut side up, on the parchment.

2 *Season the cavity* of each tomato half with a pinch of salt, a good pinch of sugar and some of the thyme leaves. Drizzle a few drops of balsamic vinegar inside each tomato half. (Hold your thumb over the bottle opening to make this easier.) Drop a slice or two of garlic in each half, and pour 1 tsp of the olive oil into each half. It will look like a lot of olive oil; that's okay.

3 *Roast the tomatoes* until they collapse and are brown around the edges, the garlic is browned, and the juices are somewhat caramelized on the sheet pan, 30 to 40 minutes. Let the tomatoes cool for a few minutes on the sheet pan. Carefully transfer them to a serving plate. (If the juices are very caramelized, the tomatoes may stick a bit; take care not to rip the skin.) Serve warm or at room temperature.

Yields 20 tomato halves; serves 6

Roasted Tomato, Basil, and Mozzarella "Sandwiches"

Put out a platter of these at your next buffet meal and watch them disappear. They make great hors d'oeuvres or antipasto, but they're delicious on a dinner plate, too.

1 RECIPE CARAMELIZED PLUM TOMATOES IN AN OLIVE OIL BATH (*page 41*), *any excess oil drained*

20 FRESH BASIL LEAVES

8 MINI-MOZZARELLA BALLS (*1 in/2.5 cm in diameter*), *each sliced into 3 to 4 pieces*

KOSHER SALT

1 *Have ready a serving platter* or shallow dish and twenty 4-in/10-cm cocktail skewers.

2 *Lay the plum tomatoes,* cut side up, on a cutting board. Place a basil leaf, shiny side down, on each tomato half. Put a piece of mozzarella on one end of the tomato and sprinkle a little salt over it. Fold the other half of the tomato over the cheese and put a skewer through the "sandwich" at an angle, so that about ¾ in/2 cm of the skewer comes out the other side. It's best to skewer through the folded-over ends of the tomato (and the cheese), but not the middle, to prevent the "sandwich" from flopping open. Arrange the tomatoes on a serving platter in diagonal rows, tucking them close to one another.

Yields 20 sandwiches; serves 6 to 8

Roasted Brussels Sprouts with Orange Butter Sauce

The trick to roasting Brussels sprouts is to first cut them in halves (if they're on the small side) or quarters (if they're a bit mature). Whole Brussels sprouts will just burn on the outside before they're cooked all the way through. I like halves because I can arrange them cut side down, which browns the bottoms and tops but keeps some of the moisture inside. For that reason, I try to choose sprouts that are on the small side; these days some of the Brussels sprouts in the store are the size of small cabbages! At any size, they deliver a delicious nutty flavor when roasted.

I make a smooth, flavorful butter sauce to dress up the roasted sprouts, but you could just drizzle them with a little melted butter and season with a squeeze of lemon. This butter sauce is also delicious on roasted broccoli. Serve the sprouts with a braised pork butt on the weekend, or a pan-seared ham steak on a weeknight. They'd also be delicious with bratwursts and beer.

1 LB/455 G SMALL BRUSSELS SPROUTS, *trimmed and halved lengthwise*

2 TBSP EXTRA-VIRGIN OLIVE OIL

½ TSP KOSHER SALT

2 TSP BALSAMIC VINEGAR

1 TBSP PURE MAPLE SYRUP

1 TBSP FRESH ORANGE JUICE

½ TSP FINELY GRATED ORANGE ZEST

2 TBSP COLD UNSALTED BUTTER, *cut into 16 pieces*

1   *Preheat the oven* to 475°F/245°C (Gas Mark 9). Line a large (18-x-13-x-1-in/45.5-x-33-x-2.5-cm) heavy-duty rimmed sheet pan with a piece of parchment paper.

2   *In a mixing bowl,* toss the Brussels sprouts with the olive oil and ½ tsp of the salt. Arrange the sprouts in one layer, cut side down, on the parchment.

3   *Roast until brown and tender,* 15 to 18 minutes. (The tops will be dark brown and crispy and the sprouts should feel tender when pierced with a paring knife.) Transfer the sprouts to a mixing bowl.

4   *Combine the balsamic vinegar,* maple syrup, orange juice, and orange zest in a small saucepan. Heat the mixture over medium heat just until it's hot (you will see a bit of steam), but not simmering. Remove the pan from the heat and add the cold butter, several pieces at a time, whisking constantly until the mixture is smooth and creamy. (Don't reheat the mixture or the butter will break and the sauce won't be creamy.) Pour the sauce over the sprouts and stir thoroughly but gently until most of the sauce has been absorbed. Transfer the sprouts and any remaining sauce to a serving platter or dinner plates.

Serves 4

Tiny Roasted Root Vegetables with Shallots and Fresh Herb Salt

Every time I make these, I get a silly kick out of seeing all the colorful little dice arranged on the parchment paper. (But then again, I'm very enthusiastic about vegetables.) These make a nice side dish on their own, or try them as a bed for steak or as part of the Warm Bistro Salad on page 47. I hold back on some of the salt before roasting, because I like to season the vegetables with a little bit of Fresh Herb Salt when they come out of the oven. (I don't do this before roasting because the heat can make herbs turn bitter or lose their flavor altogether.) A small drizzle of olive oil is nice, too.

Be sure to choose a mix of at least three or four different vegetables for color and flavor variety. I don't peel turnips, potatoes, or sweet potatoes before roasting—only carrots and parsnips. Make the herb salt while your vegetables are roasting; don't be tempted to make it hours ahead—it doesn't hold well. You can easily double this recipe if you've got two sheet pans and a little more time. (Or, if you're short on time, you can cut the vegetables into larger pieces—see the variation following this recipe.)

1 LB/455 G ROOT VEGETABLES (choose a mix of turnips, carrots, orange or white sweet potatoes, parsnips, red potatoes, and Yukon gold potatoes), cut into ¼-in/6.5-mm dice

2 TBSP PLUS 1 TSP EXTRA-VIRGIN OLIVE OIL, and more if needed

KOSHER SALT

3 OZ/85 G SHALLOTS (about 4 medium), trimmed, peeled, and cut into ¼-in-/6.5-mm-thick slices

Fresh Herb Salt (optional)

½ TSP CHOPPED FRESH ROSEMARY OR THYME

½ TSP KOSHER SALT

1   *Preheat the oven* to 475°F/245°C (Gas Mark 9). Line a large (18-x-13-x-1-in/45.5-x-33-x-2.5-cm) heavy-duty rimmed sheet pan with a piece of parchment paper.

2   *In a mixing bowl,* toss the diced vegetables with 2 Tbsp of the olive oil and ½ tsp of kosher salt. In a small bowl, coat the shallot slices, without breaking them apart, with the remaining 1 tsp olive oil and a pinch of kosher salt.

3   *Spread out the vegetables* and the shallots (keeping the rings together) in one layer on the sheet pan. (They will be somewhat crowded.) Roast until all of the vegetables are tender and some are beginning to brown around the edges (the shallots will be browned on the bottom), 22 to 24 minutes.

4   *To make the Fresh Herb Salt* (if using), combine the herbs and salt in a small bowl and mix well with your fingers. Let sit for a few minutes before using.

5   *Toss all the vegetables together,* breaking up the shallot rings, and season with up to ½ tsp of Fresh Herb Salt or a few pinches of kosher salt. Drizzle a tiny bit of olive oil over the vegetables, if you like, and toss again.

Serves 3

SIMPLE ROASTED ROOTS

If you're not in the mood for cutting small dice, but you crave the flavor of roasted roots, you can follow this recipe with a few tweaks. Skip the shallots (they will burn and taste too bitter on a less-crowded sheet pan), but increase the amount of root vegetables to 1¼ lb/570 g and cut them in larger dice (½- to ¾-in/1.25- to 2-cm pieces). The roasting time will not be much longer because there is more space between the vegetables. Check for tenderness with a paring knife after 20 to 22 minutes, but continue cooking for up to 28 minutes if you want more browning and crispness. Season with Fresh Herb Salt or kosher salt and a drizzle of olive oil, if desired.

Serves 3 to 4

Warm Bistro Salad with Tiny Roasted Root Vegetables and Bacon Dressing

If you're having friends over, this lovely winter salad could be the first course for a warming dinner of braised short ribs or lamb shanks. But if it's only the two of you some chilly night, you can simply make two large salads instead of four smaller ones and eat this for dinner with a hunk of good artisan bread and a nice young red wine. If you just want to cook the tiny roasted vegetables (they're cute), and not bother with the salad, see the recipe on page 44.

Be sure to use at least four different vegetables in this salad for a variety of colors and flavors. (Don't peel the turnips, potatoes, or sweet potatoes.) I call for a salad green called curly endive in this recipe. It is often mislabeled in the grocery store as "chicory." It is not, however, escarole, which has broader, thicker leaves; nor is it frisée, which has thinner, more delicate leaves. If you need a substitute, frisée would be a better option than escarole. Either way, serve the salad soon after dressing as it will begin to wilt fairly quickly.

Since this recipe was designed to be an alternative use for the Tiny Roasted Root Vegetables, it takes a bit more time than some. While the vegetables can be prepped and cooked in 35 to 40 minutes, washing the greens and making the salad will add on 10 to 15 minutes.

6 CUPS/95 G TORN CURLY ENDIVE, *washed and dried*

1 RECIPE TINY ROASTED ROOT VEGETABLES WITH SHALLOTS (page 44), *made without the herb salt*

2 OZ/60 G BACON, *cut into medium-small dice*

2½ TO 3 TBSP OLIVE OIL

1 TBSP PLUS 1 TSP RED-WINE VINEGAR

1¾ TSP DIJON MUSTARD

KOSHER SALT

FRESHLY GROUND BLACK PEPPER

{ Continued }

1   *Put the curly endive* in a large, heat-proof mixing bowl. Choose four salad plates and make room on your counter for plating the salads.

2   *Make the Tiny Roasted Root Vegetables,* roasting the vegetables for 18 to 22 minutes. (They don't need to be well-browned for this recipe.)

3   *In a small nonstick skillet,* cook the bacon over medium heat until crisp. With a slotted spoon, transfer the bacon to a paper towel–lined plate. Remove the pan from the heat and let cool for just a minute or two. You should have 1 to 1½ Tbsp of fat left in the pan. Add enough of the olive oil to make about 3 Tbsp total. Add 1 Tbsp of the red-wine vinegar and 1½ tsp of the Dijon mustard. (It may sputter a bit.) Whisk to combine, but don't worry if the warm vinaigrette looks "broken"—that's fine.

4   *In a mixing bowl,* season the curly endive with several good pinches of salt and a few grinds of pepper. Stir the warm vinaigrette again and pour it over the endive. Toss the endive thoroughly until it's well coated with the vinaigrette. Portion the endive onto the four salad plates. In the same mixing bowl, add 1 Tbsp olive oil, the remaining 1 tsp of red-wine vinegar, the remaining ¼ tsp of Dijon, and a pinch of salt. Stir to roughly combine. Add the roasted vegetables to the bowl and toss them with the oil and vinegar mixture (break up the shallot rings, if possible). Portion the vegetables on top of and around the endive, and garnish each salad with the crisp bacon pieces. Serve right away as the curly endive will begin to soften.

Serves 4

Eggplant and Basil "Caponata" Salad

This colorful and bright-tasting roasted vegetable salad has a secret ingredient in the dressing—cocoa. You won't know it's around—just that this tastes delicious.

A large sheet pan is especially useful for this recipe. If you don't have one, use two smaller sheet pans. This is a large amount of vegetables, and if you pile them all on one smaller pan, they will steam rather than roast.

1 GLOBE EGGPLANT *(1¼ lb/570 g), unpeeled, ends trimmed, and cut into ¾-in/2-cm dice*

1 LARGE RED BELL PEPPER *(6 to 7 oz/170 to 200 g), cored, seeded, and cut into ¾-in/2-cm pieces*

1 LARGE YELLOW OR ORANGE BELL PEPPER *(6 to 7 oz/170 to 200 g), cored, seeded, and cut into ¾-in/2-cm pieces*

⅓ CUP/75 ML PLUS 1 TSP EXTRA-VIRGIN OLIVE OIL

1¼ TSP KOSHER SALT

2 TSP FRESH LEMON JUICE

2 TSP SOY SAUCE

2 TSP DARK BROWN SUGAR

½ TSP UNSWEETENED COCOA POWDER

2 TSP FINELY CHOPPED FRESH GINGER

1½ TSP MINCED FRESH GARLIC

2 TBSP COARSELY CHOPPED FRESH PARSLEY

12 LARGE FRESH BASIL LEAVES, *torn into ¾-in/2-cm pieces*

1   *Preheat the oven* to 475°F/245°C (Gas Mark 9). Line a large (18-x-13-x-1-in/45.5-x-33-x-2.5-cm) heavy-duty rimmed sheet pan with a piece of parchment paper.

2   *In a large mixing bowl,* combine the eggplant, bell peppers, ⅓ cup/75 ml of the olive oil, and salt. Mix thoroughly, transfer to the sheet pan, and arrange the vegetables evenly in one layer. Roast the vegetables, flipping or stirring once with a spatula halfway through cooking, until the eggplant is shrunken and nicely browned, about 30 minutes. The peppers will be softened and somewhat browned on the skin side. Let cool for 5 minutes.

3   *Meanwhile, in a small bowl,* combine the lemon juice, soy sauce, brown sugar, cocoa, ginger, garlic, and the remaining 1 tsp olive oil. Whisk vigorously to mix and dissolve the cocoa. (This may take a few minutes.)

4   *Transfer the vegetables* to a large mixing bowl and drizzle the dressing over them while stirring and folding them gently with a silicone spatula. It may look like a lot of liquid, but continue to stir gently, and the vegetables will absorb most or all of it. Add the parsley and basil and stir well to incorporate. Transfer to a serving platter and serve warm or at room temperature.

Serves 6

Roasted Turnips and Pears with Rosemary-Honey Drizzle

There's a lovely balance in this autumn side dish between the sweet pears and the, well, not-so-sweet turnips, and between the floral honey and the piney rosemary. All of the flavors come together in a way that just might be palatable for people who normally wouldn't eat turnips. These would be especially good nestled next to a braised lamb shank or a piece of pot roast. Purple-topped turnips don't need peeling; nor do I peel pears when I'm roasting them, so this is an easy dish to put together.

3 MEDIUM PURPLE-TOPPED TURNIPS *(14 to 15 oz/400 to 425 g total), unpeeled, cut into ½- to ¾-in/1.25- to 2-cm dice*

1 FIRM BUT RIPE BOSC PEAR *(about 7 oz/200 g), unpeeled, cored, and cut into ½-in/1.25-cm dice*

2 TBSP VEGETABLE OIL

1 TSP KOSHER SALT

1 TBSP UNSALTED BUTTER

1 TBSP HONEY

2 TSP CHOPPED FRESH ROSEMARY

1   *Preheat the oven* to 475°F/245°C (Gas Mark 9). Line a large (18-x-13-x-1-in/45.5-x-33-x-2.5-cm) heavy-duty rimmed sheet pan with a piece of parchment paper.

2   *In a mixing bowl,* toss the turnips and pear with the vegetable oil and salt. Spread out the turnips and pear in one layer on the sheet pan. Roast, flipping with a spatula once or twice during cooking if you like, until the turnips are tender when pierced with a paring knife or spatula, 25 to 30 minutes (the turnips will be brown on some sides, the pears will be a bit darker).

3   *Meanwhile, melt the butter* in a small saucepan and add the honey and rosemary. Simmer for a few seconds and remove from the heat.

4   *Transfer the cooked turnips and pears* to a mixing bowl and drizzle the butter mixture over all, scraping all of the mixture out of the saucepan. Toss well and transfer to a serving dish.

Serves 3

Vanilla and Cardamom Glazed Acorn Squash Rings

The buttery glaze that tops these delicious squash rings is more subtly flavored than it sounds. But it adds just the right amount of sweetness and interest to the earthy flavor and silky texture of roasted acorn squash. You might be accustomed to roasting acorn squash in halves or quarters, but it's easy to quick-roast it by cutting it into pretty rings or half-rings. Because of the relatively thin slices, I find the skin perfectly edible, but it's also easy enough to eat the flesh and leave the roasted skin behind.

If you wanted to serve these for Thanksgiving, they could go in the oven when the turkey comes out, because they cook quickly. And with a second baking sheet, you can easily double or triple the recipe. Rotate the baking sheets halfway through cooking. You can also substitute delicata squash in this recipe. Because the rings will be smaller, the cooking time will be slightly shorter, so you might want to flip the rings after 8 minutes.

1 SMALL ACORN SQUASH
(1 to 1¼ lb/455 to 570 g)

2 TBSP UNSALTED BUTTER,
plus 2 tsp more if needed

2 TSP PURE MAPLE SYRUP

1½ TSP VANILLA EXTRACT

⅛ TSP GROUND CARDAMOM

KOSHER SALT

1   *Preheat the oven* to 475°F/245°C (Gas Mark 9). Line a large (18-x-13-x-1-in/45.5-x-33-x-2.5-cm) heavy-duty rimmed sheet pan with a piece of parchment paper.

{ Continued }

2 *With a sharp chef's knife,* cut the acorn squash in half lengthwise (through both the stem end and the pointy end). Scrape out the seeds and fibers with a spoon. Put each half, cut side down, on a cutting board. Slice off about ¾ in/2 cm from each end, and discard. Slice the squash crosswise into ½-in-/1.25-cm-thick half-rings. If you want, you can trim away any remaining fibers from the rings by running a paring knife around the inside of each. Put the half-rings on the parchment paper.

3 *In a small saucepan,* melt the 2 Tbsp butter over low heat. Remove the pan from the heat and add the maple syrup, vanilla, and cardamom. Stir well. Use a pastry brush to lightly brush the squash pieces with a little less than half of the mixture. Season the pieces very lightly with salt and turn them over. Brush this side with more of the mixture, but reserve about 1 Tbsp for brushing on after cooking. (If using a larger squash and you wind up with a little bit less than 1 Tbsp of liquid, add 1 or 2 tsp more butter to the saucepan.) Season the tops very lightly with salt.

4 *Roast the squash* for 12 minutes. Use tongs to flip the pieces over. Continue to roast until they are nicely browned (the bottoms will be browner then the tops) and tender when pierced with a paring knife, 10 to 12 minutes. Flip the pieces over again when they come out of the oven so that the browner side is up.

5 *Reheat the butter mixture* briefly over low heat if necessary (or to melt the additional butter). Brush the butter mixture over the squash slices and serve.

Serves 2 or 3

Tip: **To cut whole squash rings, trim away about ¾ in/2 cm of both ends of the squash and carefully slice it crosswise into ½-in/1.25-cm rings. Run a paring knife around the insides of the rings to remove excess fibers.**

Chapter 4

Quick-Braising

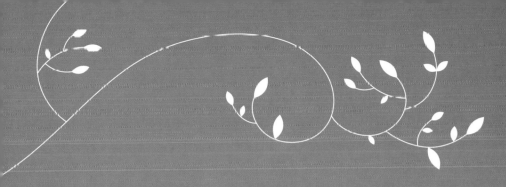

METHOD: Quick-braising

EQUIPMENT: 10-in/25-cm straight-sided sauté pan with lid, tongs, silicone spatula, wooden spoon

HEAT: The stove top, starting high and turning down to low

....

Braising: How It Works

Braising may just be my favorite cooking method, because it delivers the best of both worlds—browning for deep flavor, simmering for tender texture. You're probably familiar with braising as a great way to cook tough meats like lamb shanks and short ribs as well as meat for pot roast. After a serious sear on the stove top to give the meat a beautiful brown exterior, liquids and aromatics are added to the pot, and the meat simmers, on the stove top or in the oven, very slowly until really tender. I know, this doesn't sound like something you'd want to do to your fresh, delicate vegetables—or that you'd have time for, either. But humor me here for a minute.

For weeknight vegetables, you take the same idea and just shorten the cooking times and liquid amounts radically. A very quick sear in a sauté pan, followed by a simmer in a very small amount of liquid, produces vegetables with rich flavor that are perfectly cooked through, pleasantly moist, and lightly sauced. Because the vegetables—think green beans, asparagus, broccoli, carrots—get browned first, they produce some yummy browned bits on the bottom of the pan. Those in turn add a lot of flavor to the finished dish when the pan is deglazed by that little bit of liquid.

I first developed my version of this quick-braising technique for an article I did for *Fine Cooking* magazine several years ago. And I have to tell you, a lot of my coworkers (and our readers!) wound up adding quick-braising to their weeknight repertoires. So please don't be intimidated if you've never tried this before. I'll give you a few tips before you get started, and then you might want to dive in and just try one of the recipes from the list on page 55. But don't forget that you can always go back to the foundation recipe on page 58 on a night when you just have a bunch of carrots you're looking to cook. I've kept the ingredients list short and the flavors simpler in the foundation recipe, so that you don't get overwhelmed with too many choices. But once you get the hang of the technique, feel free to embellish the foundation recipe with flavor ideas from the other recipes or to combine two or more vegetables in one braise.

For the best results with any of the recipes, be sure to cut your vegetables into small or medium-size pieces (no large chunks) so that they can cook through quickly and evenly. Long, narrow vegetables like green beans and asparagus are perfect for this method, as they hardly need more than a trim. I like to cut vegetables like carrots into sticks, not coins, because sticks have more browning area and also tend not to smother each other like coin shapes do. Try to cut other veggies in consistenly sized pieces, not because they'll look pretty, but because they'll cook more evenly. Then, be sure that your vegetables are all in one layer on the bottom of the pan. That way, every piece of vegetable gets a chance to brown by being in contact with the pan. Also, overcrowding the pan would mean some vegetables would not get cooked through during the simmering stage.

Before you even turn on your stove to make one of these recipes, please buy a good-quality straight-sided sauté pan! I am a firm believer in the promise that good equipment will give good results, and this workhorse pan is incredibly versatile. What I call a 10-inch pan is usually labeled a "3-qt/3-L" pan, so there can be some slight differences in width and depth. I am partial to my All-Clad, which is about 10½ in/26.5 cm wide and 2½ in/6.5 cm deep. Whatever brand you buy, be sure you're getting a three-ply pan with a stainless-steel exterior and interior (not nonstick) and an aluminum or copper core.

You'll notice that I use a few different utensils for handling vegetables in these recipes. First, I find tongs (short, comfortable ones) easiest for turning and flipping vegetables. Then, I will sometimes use a wooden spoon to scrape up browned bits from the bottom of the pan. But more often these days, I find that one of those colorful heat-proof silicone spatulas does a good job of stirring in sauce ingredients and incorporating browned bits at the end.

There's one last piece of equipment that I use constantly when making these recipes—a scale. Weighing awkwardly shaped vegetables is a lot more accurate than trying to pack them in cups; so you'll have better control over the end results if you can weigh your veggies. And once you buy a scale, you'll find you use it a lot for baking and other savory recipes, too. If this seems like a bother, at least try using the scale, the first few times you make a recipe; after that you might get good at eye-balling what amounts work.

VEGETABLES FOR QUICK-BRAISING

VEGETABLE	WAY TO CUT
Asparagus	cut into medium-thick spears, tough ends trimmed so that all spears are 6 to 7 in/15.25 to 17.75 cm long
Broccoli crowns	cut into medium florets, halved, each piece with one flat side
*Brussels sprouts**	trimmed, halved
Carrots	peeled, tops and tails trimmed, cut into sticks 2 to 3 in/5 to 7.5 cm long and about ⅜ in/9.5 mm wide
Cauliflower florets	cut into medium florets, halved, each piece with one flat side
Green beans	stem ends trimmed
Parsnips	peeled, cut into sticks about 3 in/7.5 cm long and about ½ in/1.25 cm wide
*Potatoes, baby or slim fingerling**	halved

*Add 2 to 3 Tbsp more liquid for these vegetables.

Foundation Recipe for Quick-Braising

You will feel like Houdini once you learn to improvise braised vegetables on a weeknight, because they deliver such amazing flavor in less than 30 minutes. The technique's not hard; it's just that you'll need to pay close attention to a few things the first couple of times you do this. The reason: The cooking times in this recipe are dependent on the heat of your own individual stove top and, to a lesser degree, the brand of pan you use. So you'll want to use the cooking times and the amount of liquid I suggest as guidelines—you can always lower the heat if your veggies are browning too fast, or add a little more liquid if they don't feel tender enough after the liquid reduces. In most cases ⅓ cup/75 ml of liquid will work fine, but I've suggested adding a few more tablespoons when cooking the Brussels sprouts or potatoes, which are fairly dense. If you do not want to use chicken broth, you could use half vegetable broth and half water. The recipe would work, too, with all water. The sauce would not have the gloss that broth gives it, but the dish will still be flavorful.

Once you get on a roll, you can combine two or more vegetables in the same braise (such as carrots, green beans, and asparagus together or broccoli and cauliflower together), as long as you keep the total weight the same and don't overcrowd the pan. And you can customize this recipe by trying a few variations. Start the sauté by crisping up some pancetta, add ginger or garlic, mix a bit of wine or juice with the chicken broth, or replace the last bit of butter with cream.

Before you start cooking, be sure that your sauté pan has a lid. If you can't find a lid, you can use the bottom of another sauté pan (of the same size or larger) to cover your pan.

12 OZ TO 1 LB/340 TO 455 G YOUR CHOICE OF VEGETABLE *(10 to 12 oz/285 to 340 g trimmed; see the table on page 58 for choices and how to cut them)*

1 TBSP EXTRA-VIRGIN OLIVE OIL

1½ TBSP UNSALTED BUTTER

½ TSP KOSHER SALT

⅓ CUP/80 ML LOW-SODIUM CHICKEN BROTH *(more for some vegetables)*

1 TO 2 TSP FRESH LEMON OR LIME JUICE

2 TSP CHOPPED FRESH PARSLEY, CILANTRO, MINT, OR TARRAGON *(optional)*

1   *Spread out the vegetables* in a 10-in/25-cm straight-sided sauté pan to see if they fit in one layer with just a little bit of overlapping. If you have too many, put some aside to use another night.

2   *Heat the olive oil* and 1 Tbsp of the butter in the sauté pan over medium-high heat. When the butter has melted and is beginning to foam, add the vegetables and salt and toss well with tongs. Arrange the vegetables in one layer. Cook, without stirring, until the bottoms are nicely browned, 3 to 5 minutes. Turn over, and cook for another 2 to 4 minutes to lightly brown another side.

3   *Reduce the heat* to medium-low, pour in the broth, immediately cover the pan, and simmer until the liquid reduces to 1 to 2 Tbsp, 2 to 3 minutes. The vegetables should be just tender enough to pierce with a fork.

4   *Uncover the pan,* reduce the heat to medium-low and add the lemon juice and the remaining ½ Tbsp butter. Toss gently with a silicone spatula just until the butter melts, scraping any browned bits from the bottom of the pan. Remove the pan from the heat, stir in the herbs (if using), and transfer the vegetables to a serving dish. Pour the pan sauce over them, scraping it all out of the pan.

Serves 3

Quick-Braised Asparagus with Dijon, White Wine, and Fresh Thyme Pan Sauce

I won't fool you; these asparagus look a bit rustic. But the browning in this recipe (as in so many others in this book) pays off with deep flavor. The glazy pan sauce cloaks the asparagus in even more flavor, and this is one tasty dish. It's a quick one, too—easy to do in less than 30 minutes. Serve it with pork tenderloin and couscous on a weeknight or sear-roasted pork loin and a grain pilaf on a weekend.

This method works best with asparagus that are of equal thickness—medium or just slightly larger than medium. "Pencils" will overcook. You can do this with jumbos, as long as most of the woody stem is cut off and you add on an extra minute of browning. Whether the asparagus is medium or thick, just be sure that the pan is not overcrowded so that each piece can make contact with the pan surface for browning. For this one, you'll definitely want your tongs handy for flipping the asparagus over. Also, cover the pan as soon as you pour in the little bit of liquid; it reduces quickly, and it's the steam—captured by the lid—that finishes cooking the asparagus.

¼ CUP/60 ML LOW-SODIUM CHICKEN BROTH

2 TBSP DRY WHITE WINE, *such as Sauvignon Blanc*

1 TBSP EXTRA-VIRGIN OLIVE OIL

1 TBSP UNSALTED BUTTER

1 BUNCH MEDIUM-THICK ASPARAGUS, *trimmed to 6-in/15.25-cm lengths (yielding about 10 oz/285 g)*

¼ TSP KOSHER SALT

1 TSP ROUGHLY CHOPPED FRESH THYME

½ TSP DIJON MUSTARD

1   *Combine the broth* and white wine in a liquid measuring cup.

2   *In a 10-in/25-cm straight-sided sauté pan* with a lid, heat the olive oil and ½ Tbsp of the butter over medium-high heat. When the butter has melted and is bubbling, add the asparagus and salt and toss well to coat. Arrange in one layer and cook, without stirring, until the undersides are nicely browned, about 4 minutes.

3   *Using tongs,* turn over each spear and cook, without stirring, just until the other side is beginning to brown, about 2 minutes. Carefully (it will sputter) pour the liquid into the pan and immediately cover it. Simmer until the liquid reduces almost completely (1 or 2 tsp will be left), about 2 minutes. Uncover, remove the pan from the heat, and add the remaining ½ Tbsp of butter, the thyme, and mustard. Stir gently with a silicone spatula to mix the mustard with the melting butter and to incorporate any browned bits from the bottom of the pan. Transfer the asparagus to a serving platter or plates and pour the pan sauce over it, scraping all of the sauce out of the pan.

Serves 3

Quick-Braised Green Beans with Pomegranate-Balsamic Pan Sauce

The trick to making the silky pan sauce for these beans is to reduce the pomegranate-balsamic mixture to a syrupy consistency, and then add cold butter. By adding the butter at the last minute off the heat, it will melt just enough to make the sauce creamy and coat the beans. Once the butter's melted, don't put the pan back on the stove. Further heat will break the creamy emulsion. I like to transfer the beans and sauce to a serving dish as soon as they're done; it prevents the sauce from continuing to cook.

Because I like to drink pomegranate juice and use it in sauces, I usually keep a bottle of it in my fridge (I like both POM and Odwalla brands). But if you don't usually keep this juice on hand, and you find you want to make quick-braised green beans some weeknight, you could substitute orange juice.

1 TBSP POMEGRANATE JUICE	12 OZ/340 G GREEN BEANS, TRIMMED
1 TSP BALSAMIC VINEGAR	¾ TSP KOSHER SALT
1 TSP PURE MAPLE SYRUP	⅓ CUP/80 ML LOW-SODIUM CHICKEN BROTH
½ TSP MINCED FRESH GINGER	
2 TBSP UNSALTED BUTTER	2 TBSP COARSELY CHOPPED TOASTED PECANS *(see tip on page 36)*
1 TBSP EXTRA-VIRGIN OLIVE OIL	

1   *Combine the pomegranate juice,* balsamic vinegar, maple syrup, and ginger in a small bowl. Cut 1 Tbsp of the butter into 6 pieces and keep them chilled in the refrigerator.

2   *In a 10-in/25 cm straight-sided sauté pan* with a lid, heat the olive oil and the remaining 1 Tbsp of butter over medium-high heat. When the butter has melted and is starting to foam, add the green beans and salt and toss to coat well. Using tongs, arrange the green beans in the pan so that as many beans as possible are touching the bottom. Cook, without stirring, until the bottoms are browned, about 4 minutes.

3   *Stir the beans,* turning over as many as possible, and cook, arranging the beans as necessary, until most of the beans are lightly browned and feel more pliable, about 4 minutes more. Carefully pour the broth into the pan (it will sputter, but don't turn down the heat). Cover and cook until all but 1 or 2 Tbsp of the liquid has evaporated (uncover once or twice and swirl the liquid to distribute if necessary), 3 to 4 minutes. Uncover the pan, add the pomegranate juice mixture, and cook, stirring, until it reduces to a syrupy consistency, about 1 minute. (It will bubble quite a bit and lighten in color.) Remove the pan from the heat and add the cold pieces of butter. Stir well with a rubber spatula until the butter is melted and the sauce is creamy. Transfer the beans and sauce to a serving platter or dinner plates and garnish with the toasted pecans.

Serves 3

Gingery Braised Brussels Sprouts

Quick-braising is one of my favorite ways to cook Brussels sprouts, because browning them first and then simmering them just until done gives them a nutty flavor and a perfect texture. I highly recommend you try this buttery, gingery version on your friends who don't think they like these little green vegetables. Serve them (the vegetables, not the friends) with smashed potatoes and slices of baked ham or roast pork loin.

Brussels sprouts seem to range in size all over the map these days. I think this is because they're being grown—and harvested—year-round, and sometimes they're very mature, almost like mini-cabbages. The amount of liquid in this recipe is designed to be just enough to cook medium-size sprouts that have been cut in half, but it will be fine for slightly larger sprouts, too. If your sprouts are huge or very tiny, adjust the chicken broth up or down by 2 Tbsp. Whatever you do, don't skip that bit of butter at the end; we're erring here on the side of being just a little bit decadent. And don't skimp on the ginger.

2½ TBSP UNSALTED BUTTER

1 TBSP EXTRA-VIRGIN OLIVE OIL

12 TO 13 OZ/340 TO 370 G BRUSSELS SPROUTS, *trimmed and halved*

¾ TSP KOSHER SALT

½ CUP/120 ML LOW-SODIUM CHICKEN BROTH

1 TBSP MINCED FRESH GINGER

1 TSP MINCED FRESH GARLIC

½ SMALL LIME

1   *In a 10-in/25-cm straight-sided sauté pan* with a lid, melt 1½ Tbsp of the butter with the olive oil over medium heat. Arrange the Brussels sprouts, cut side down, in one layer in the pan. (You'll have to tuck them in snugly.) Season with the salt. Cook the sprouts until the bottoms are nicely browned, 4 to 6 minutes. (If the heat on your stove top is uneven, rotate the pan so that the bottoms become evenly browned.) Pour the broth into the pan and cover, leaving the lid slightly askew so that some steam escapes. Turn the heat down if necessary so that the broth is just gently simmering.

2   *Cook until the broth* is reduced to about 2 Tbsp, 7 to 9 minutes. Remove the lid and add the remaining 1 Tbsp butter, the ginger, and garlic. Toss well and stir just until the butter has melted. Remove the pan from the heat and continue to stir gently until the ginger and garlic are well incorporated and slightly softened. Gently squeeze the lime half over all, toss, and serve.

Serves 4

Cider-Braised Baby Bok Choy and Golden Apples

Baby bok choy is one of my favorite vegetables, though I wish it were around the markets more. Snatch some up when you see it. Quick-braising is a wonderful way to cook baby bok choy, because browning it first accentuates its sweeter side, and simmering it leaves the texture perfectly balanced between crunchy and tender.

Since baby bok choy is a member of the cabbage family (though a mild one), I thought to pair it up with apples and a little bit of apple cider in this quick-braise. It turned out to be a lovely combination. If you have a choice, choose the smallest, most slender vegetables (of equal size). I sometimes see "baby" bok choy that is more like "teenage" bok choy. Larger bok choy will not cook properly with the cooking times and amount of liquid suggested in this recipe. You'll probably need to wash the bok choy to get out the bits of grit hiding between the lower stalks.

I like these so much that sometimes I just make the whole recipe for myself and eat it with a bowl of brown rice.

3 TBSP LOW-SODIUM CHICKEN BROTH

2 TBSP APPLE CIDER

½ TSP SOY SAUCE

1 TBSP EXTRA-VIRGIN OLIVE OIL

1 TBSP UNSALTED BUTTER

¼ TSP KOSHER SALT

2 BABY BOK CHOY *(6 to 7 in/15.25 to 17.75 cm long, 2 in/5 cm wide, weighing about 8 oz/225 g), halved lengthwise, washed, and spun dry*

½ LARGE GOLDEN DELICIOUS APPLE *(about 4 oz/115 g), cored and cut into 8 wedges*

¼ TSP GRATED FRESH GINGER

1 | *Combine the broth,* cider, and soy sauce in a liquid measuring cup.

2 | *In a 10-in/25-cm straight-sided sauté pan* with a lid, heat the olive oil and ½ Tbsp of the butter over medium heat. When the butter has melted and is bubbling, sprinkle the salt over the pan. Arrange the bok choy, cut side down, and the apple wedges in one layer in the pan. Cook, without stirring, until the undersides of the bok choy and the apples are nicely browned, 6 to 7 minutes.

3 | *With tongs,* gently turn the apple wedges over. Carefully pour the liquid into the pan and cover immediately. Simmer until the liquid is almost completely reduced (1 or 2 tsp will be left), 5 to 6 minutes. Uncover, remove the pan from the heat, and transfer the bok choy and the apples to a serving platter. Add the remaining ½ Tbsp butter and the ginger to the pan and stir well with a silicone spatula as the butter melts, scraping up any browned bits from the bottom of the pan. Pour the sauce over the bok choy and apples, scraping it out of the pan.

Serves 4

Braised Carrots with Blood Orange–Fresh Tarragon Pan Sauce

The pan sauce for these carrots has a silky texture and a slightly sweet licorice flavor from the mingling of the fresh tarragon and the blood orange; it works beautifully to smooth out the mineral-y edge of carrots. If you can't find blood oranges (they're in season November through March), you can use navel oranges or tangerines for the zest and juice, or you could also replace some or all of the juice with pomegranate or cranberry juice. For a small holiday gathering, these carrots would make a nice addition to a main course of filet mignon and perhaps a potato gratin like the Golden Mushroom and Potato Gratin on page 198.

½ TSP FINELY GRATED BLOOD ORANGE ZEST

1 TBSP BLOOD ORANGE JUICE

2 TSP PURE MAPLE SYRUP

1 TSP RED-WINE VINEGAR

1½ TBSP UNSALTED BUTTER

1 TBSP EXTRA-VIRGIN OLIVE OIL

1 LB/455 G CARROTS, *peeled and cut into sticks about 3 in/7.5 cm long and ⅜ in/9.5 mm thick*

¾ TSP KOSHER SALT

¼ CUP/60 ML LOW-SODIUM CHICKEN BROTH

2 TSP FINELY CHOPPED FRESH TARRAGON

1 *Combine the blood orange zest and juice,* maple syrup, and vinegar in a small bowl and set aside. Cut ½ Tbsp of the butter into 4 pieces and keep them chilled in the refrigerator.

2 *In a 10-in/25-cm straight-sided sauté pan* with a lid, heat the remaining 1 Tbsp butter with the olive oil over medium-high heat. When the butter has melted, add the carrots and salt and toss well. Arrange the carrots in mostly one layer across the bottom of the pan. Cook, without stirring, until the bottoms of the carrots are lightly browned, about 5 minutes. Stir and flip the carrots with tongs (don't worry if you don't turn them all over at first) and cook, flipping and turning the carrots occasionally, until they are all starting to feel limp and are a bit browned on at least two sides (some will be darker brown), another 5 minutes. The pan will have darkened a bit.

3 *Carefully pour the broth* into the pan (it will sputter), cover quickly, and cook until all but 1 to 2 Tbsp of the liquid has evaporated, 1 to 2 minutes. Uncover, reduce the heat to medium-low, and add the blood orange mixture and the cold butter. Using a silicone spatula, gently toss and stir, scraping any browned bits off the bottom of the pan, until the butter has melted and the pan sauce is coating the carrots, 30 seconds to 1 minute. Remove the pan from the heat, stir in the tarragon, and serve.

Serves 3 or 4

Summer Vegetable Ragout with Zucchini, Green Beans, and Corn

A bit like an elegant succotash, this fresh summer medley has a nice hit of lemon to brighten it up. It takes some time to prep these vegetables, but the cooking goes quickly—the "braise" is really just a quick reduction of chicken stock and a little bit of cream to bring everything together. The vegetables don't get overcooked, and so they retain a nice texture. This ragout is good slightly warm, as well as hot, so it can sit a bit while you put the rest of your dinner together.

Baby zucchini (about ¾ in/2 cm thick) are pretty widely available now, and a snap to prepare because you just slice across them. But if you can't find them, just cut slim zucchini into quarters lengthwise and then slice across. To finish this dish, I like to combine three or four different tender herbs (whatever you've got, as long as some of them are mild like parsley—a tablespoon of thyme would be overwhelming). They all go well with the summer vegetables and lemon. This would be nice as a bed for a sautéed crab cake. When I'm in the mood for Thai flavors, I use the vegetables and proportions in this recipe but make a few flavor changes. Instead of heavy cream, I use coconut milk. Instead of lemon, use lime. I add a little chopped lemongrass and use mint and cilantro for my herbs.

1 TSP FRESH LEMON JUICE

½ TSP FINELY GRATED LEMON ZEST

¼ TSP WORCESTERSHIRE SAUCE

¼ CUP/60 ML LOW-SODIUM CHICKEN BROTH

2 TBSP HEAVY CREAM

1 TBSP CANOLA OIL

1 CUP (about 4 oz/115 g) FRESH CORN KERNELS (from about 2 large ears; see tip)

¾ CUP (about 3½ oz/100 g) SLICED BABY ZUCCHINI (¼-in/6.5-mm pieces)

¾ CUP (about 3½ oz/100 g) SLICED SLENDER GREEN OR YELLOW WAX BEANS (¼-in/6.5-mm pieces; see tip)

1 CUP (about 4 oz/115 g) MEDIUM-DICED YELLOW ONION

½ TSP KOSHER SALT

½ TSP FINELY CHOPPED FRESH GARLIC

1 TBSP CHOPPED FRESH HERBS (a combination of parsley or chervil, chives, thyme, mint, and/or basil)

FRESHLY GROUND BLACK PEPPER

{ Continued }

1   *Combine the lemon juice,* lemon zest, and Worcestershire sauce in a small bowl. In a liquid measure, combine the broth and heavy cream. Set these aside.

2   *In a 10-in/25-cm straight-sided sauté pan* with a lid, heat the canola oil over medium-high heat. Add the corn, zucchini, green beans, onion, and salt. Cook, stirring frequently, until the bottom of the pan is browned (this is from the starch in the corn) and some of the vegetables are just beginning to brown, 4 to 6 minutes. Add the garlic and cook, stirring, just until well combined. Turn the heat to low, add the broth-cream mixture, stir well to scrape up the browned bits from the bottom of the pan, and cover. Simmer, stirring once, until the liquids have reduced to 1 or 2 Tbsp, 3 to 4 minutes. (Depending on your stove, this may go more quickly.)

3   *Remove the pan from the heat,* uncover, and stir in the lemon juice mixture and most of the fresh herbs. Season with pepper and stir again. Transfer to a serving dish or individual serving bowls and garnish with the remaining herbs.

Serves 4

Tips: I find the safest way to cut corn off the cob is to snap the shucked ears in half first. Then put one half, cut side facing down, on a large cutting board and slice down the cob with a sharp knife using a sawing motion. Keep turning the cob until you've cut off all the kernels. Repeat with the other half. For convenience, I also put a large (old) dish towel over my cutting board before I start. When I'm done cutting, I can fold in the corners of the towel and easily transfer the kernels to a bowl. Any way you do it, be aware that corn kernels do have a tendency to go flying when you cut them.

To prep the green beans, trim the ends and slice them crosswise into pieces about the size of large peas.

Creole Vegetable Ragout with Corn, Okra, and Cherry Tomatoes

This colorful dish tastes like it was cooked for a long time, but it has the texture of a nice sauté. In other words, it's a classy take on a vegetable stew. It looks lovely in a white bowl, and a few seared shrimp on top would absolutely make dinner. The sliced serranos give it a pretty nice kick of heat; you can use fewer slices if you like.

Anytime you sauté corn, its starch immediately starts to brown on the bottom of the pan. Don't be alarmed by this; just be sure to scrape all that tasty stuff up when you add the liquids. And if you've never cooked with okra, this is a great way to try it. You'll be surprised at how quickly you can prep it (just slice across), and how pretty it looks. In this dish, the texture stays firm, and the slightly sticky substance that the okra contains simply blends in with the other ingredients. By the way, okra's flavor will remind you of green beans. Look for okra pods that are firm and bright green. Choose smaller ones if you can.

1 TSP FRESH LEMON JUICE	1 CUP/100 G LARGE-DICED YELLOW ONION
¼ TSP WORCESTERSHIRE SAUCE	½ TSP KOSHER SALT
1 TBSP CANOLA OIL	1 TSP FINELY CHOPPED FRESH GARLIC
1 TBSP UNSALTED BUTTER	6 VERY THIN SLICES SERRANO PEPPER (*with seeds*)
1 CUP/85 G THINLY SLICED TRIMMED OKRA	¾ CUP/115 G QUARTERED SMALL CHERRY TOMATOES
¾ CUP/100 G FRESH CORN KERNELS (*from about 2 medium ears; for cutting tip, see page 67*)	⅓ CUP/80 ML LOW-SODIUM CHICKEN BROTH
¼ CUP/35 G SMALL-DICED RED BELL PEPPER	1 TBSP CHOPPED FRESH BASIL

1   *Combine the lemon juice* and Worcestershire sauce in a small bowl and set aside.

2   *In a 10-in/25-cm straight-sided sauté pan* with a lid, heat the canola oil and butter over medium heat. When the butter has melted, add the okra, corn, bell pepper, onion, and salt. Cook, stirring frequently, until the bottom of the pan is browned and the onion is partially translucent, about 8 minutes. Add the garlic and the serrano and cook, stirring, just until well combined. Add the cherry tomatoes and the broth, stir, turn the heat to low, and cover. Simmer until the onion is translucent and the liquid is a rich brownish orange, about 5 minutes.

3   *Uncover,* and if there is a lot of liquid in the pan, turn the heat to high, and simmer to reduce the liquid to 1 or 2 Tbsp, 1 to 2 minutes. Add the lemon juice mixture and the basil and stir well. Transfer to a shallow serving dish or individual shallow bowls.

Serves 4

Crisp-Tender Broccoflower with Lemon-Dijon Pan Sauce and Toasted Parmigiano Bread Crumbs

A broccoflower floret is a beautiful thing—plump and bright green—so it's painful to slice one. But please do. Each of your florets should be about 2 in/5 cm long and around 1 in/2.5 cm wide, so make one or two cuts through the middle of the larger florets to create consistently sized pieces with at least one flat side on each for more contact with the bottom of the pan.

This brown-and-braise method yields perfectly cooked, crisp-tender broccoflower with a lemony, buttery pan sauce, which everyone will like. The Toasted Parmigiano Bread Crumbs aren't absolutely necessary, but they don't take long to make and add a wonderful texture. This recipe also works with cauliflower; use about 12 oz/340 g.

For a vegetarian main dish, serve this over angel hair pasta tossed in a little brown butter and seasoned with lots of fresh pepper. For a slightly heartier pasta dish, add crisp pancetta before the broccoflower.

Toasted Parmigiano Bread Crumbs (optional)

½ TBSP UNSALTED BUTTER

¼ CUP/15 G FRESH BREAD CRUMBS *(see tip)*

KOSHER SALT

1 TBSP FINELY GRATED PARMIGIANO-REGGIANO *(see tip)*

1 TSP CHOPPED FRESH PARSLEY

1 TBSP EXTRA-VIRGIN OLIVE OIL

1½ TBSP UNSALTED BUTTER

10 OZ/285 G BROCCOFLOWER FLORETS, *each 2 in/5 cm long with one flat side (from about ½ head)*

½ TSP KOSHER SALT

⅓ CUP/80 ML LOW-SODIUM CHICKEN BROTH

1½ TSP FRESH LEMON JUICE

1 TSP DIJON MUSTARD

1 TSP CHOPPED FRESH PARSLEY

{ Continued }

1　*To make the Toasted Parmigiano Bread Crumbs,* melt the butter over low heat in a small nonstick skillet. Add the bread crumbs and a pinch of salt and stir well. Raise the heat to medium and cook the crumbs, stirring frequently, until they're toasted and most of them are a light golden brown, 3 to 4 minutes. Transfer to a small plate and let cool. Combine with the Parmigiano and parsley.

2　*In a 10-in/25-cm straight-sided sauté pan* with a lid, heat the olive oil and 1 Tbsp of the butter over medium-high heat. When the butter has melted and is starting to foam, add the broccoflower and salt and toss with tongs to coat. Arrange the broccoflower with one cut side down and cook without stirring until the bottoms are browned, 3 to 4 minutes. (The browning will be spotty but will be a fairly dark brown color.) Turn the florets onto another side and cook again without stirring until that side is lightly browned in spots, about 2 minutes. Carefully pour the broth into the pan (it will sputter), cover, and cook until all but 1 or 2 Tbsp of the liquid has evaporated (uncover once or twice and swirl the liquid to distribute if necessary), 2 to 3 minutes.

3　*Remove the pan from the heat,* uncover, and add the lemon juice, mustard, and the remaining ½ Tbsp butter. Stir well with a silicone spatula as the butter melts and the sauce becomes creamy. Toss in the parsley, stir, and transfer the vegetables and sauce to a serving platter or dinner plates. Garnish with the Toasted Parmigiano Bread Crumbs, if desired. (You may not need all of them. Add them immediately before serving to keep them crisp.)

Serves 3 to 4

Tips: I like to use English muffins for bread crumbs. I rip several of them into big pieces and whiz them in the food processor (or even in a coffee grinder). Then I store them in the freezer. They defrost in minutes.

A rasp-style grater (such as a Microplane) works well for finely grating Parmigiano.

Braised Fingerlings with Rosemary and Mellow Garlic

Fingerlings. Just the name of these potatoes tickles me, and then there's that great knobby shape. They're fun to cook with, and because they're relatively high in starch, braising is a great way to treat them. The starch helps them to brown up quickly in the pan, but the braising liquid keeps their fluffy texture from drying out.

2 TBSP EXTRA-VIRGIN OLIVE OIL

8 LARGE GARLIC CLOVES, *each peeled and cut crosswise into 2 or 3 pieces*

½ TSP KOSHER SALT, *and more as needed*

12 OZ/340 G SMALL FINGERLING POTATOES, *halved lengthwise*

½ CUP/120 ML LOW-SODIUM CHICKEN BROTH, *and more if necessary*

1 TBSP UNSALTED BUTTER

2 TSP FINELY CHOPPED FRESH ROSEMARY

FRESHLY GROUND BLACK PEPPER

½ TO 1 TSP SHERRY VINEGAR

1 *In a 10-in/25-cm straight-sided sauté pan* with a lid, heat the olive oil over medium heat, add the garlic, and sauté just until the oil becomes fragrant, 2 to 3 minutes. Sprinkle the salt over the bottom of the pan and arrange the potato halves, cut side down, in the pan among the garlic. Cover the pan loosely, leaving the lid partially askew to let a little steam escape, and cook until the bottoms of the potatoes are nicely browned, 7 to 9 minutes. (Move the pan around occasionally for even browning.)

2 *Pour in the broth* (it will sputter a bit), partially cover again, and reduce the heat to maintain a gentle simmer. Cook, without stirring, until the broth reduces to 1 or 2 Tbsp, 5 to 7 minutes. Pierce a potato with a paring knife. It should be just tender. (If not, add ¼ cup/60 ml cup of broth or water to the pan, partially cover, bring to a simmer, and cook until reduced to 1 or 2 Tbsp. Check again.) Add the butter and rosemary to the pan and stir the vegetables. Cook until the butter has melted and the rosemary has softened a bit and released its aroma, 1 to 2 minutes. As the butter melts, stir and scrape the bottom of the pan to incorporate any browned bits. Season the potatoes with a little more salt and pepper, and season with sherry vinegar to taste. Transfer the vegetables to a serving dish and stir and scrape out any remaining pan sauce over them. Serve warm.

Serves 3 to 4

Silky Braised Fennel in Pink Sauce

I know I probably sound like a broken record (well, that dates me!), but fennel is yet another vegetable that really benefits from this quick-braising technique. Browning it first amps up its sweet anise flavor, and simmering it softens its tough texture to a perfectly pleasant al dente. Add a touch of cream to that, and . . . yum. Here I decided to appropriate pink pasta sauce (tomato, cream, and vodka) and use it on fennel, because tomatoes and fennel go together so well. I love the richness of this dish. For some reason, I adore it with roast chicken, though it would be a natural with pork loin or lamb, too. I've added a lighter, lemony variation on braised fennel at the end of this recipe, so that you'll be sure to give this treatment a try, even if slightly rich food is not your thing.

Fennel bulbs vary a lot in size, but you will usually be able to find a large one at the grocery store. If the fennel bulbs look small, buy two just to be sure. The recipe works best with the fennel wedges covering the bottom of the pan.

¾ CUP/175 ML LOW-SODIUM CHICKEN BROTH

2 TBSP VODKA

¼ CUP/60 ML HEAVY CREAM

2 TSP TOMATO PASTE

1 LARGE FENNEL BULB (*about 1 lb 5 oz/ 600 g with stalks attached*)

2 TBSP UNSALTED BUTTER

1 TBSP EXTRA-VIRGIN OLIVE OIL

1 TSP KOSHER SALT

FRESHLY GROUND BLACK PEPPER

1   *Combine the broth* and vodka in a liquid measure and set aside. In a small bowl, whisk together the heavy cream and tomato paste and set aside.

2   *Cut the stalks off the fennel.* Chop enough of the fennel fronds to yield 1 tsp; set aside. Trim any brown spots from the outside of the bulb and cut the bulb in half. Notch most of the core out from both halves, leaving a bit of it to hold the wedges together. (You should have about 1 lb/455 g of fennel remaining.) Cut each fennel half into 6 thick wedges.

3 *In a 10-in/25-cm straight-sided sauté pan* with a lid, melt the butter with the olive oil over medium heat. Arrange the fennel wedges, one cut side down, in one layer in the pan. Season with the salt and a few grinds of pepper. Cook until the fennel wedges are nicely browned, 7 to 8 minutes. (If the heat on your burner is uneven, rotate the pan so that all the wedges brown evenly.) Turn the wedges over to another cut side with tongs. Pour the broth and vodka mixture over the fennel. Cover the pan, leaving the lid slightly askew so that some steam escapes. Make sure the liquid is gently simmering (turn the heat down or up if necessary), and cook until the liquid is reduced to just a few tablespoons, 10 to 12 minutes. Remove the lid, add the tomato-cream mixture, and cook, gently turning the fennel wedges with tongs, and stirring and scraping the bottom of the pan, until the cream thickens and coats the fennel, about 2 minutes.

4 *Remove the pan from the heat.* Serve the fennel and sauce right away, garnished with the chopped fennel fronds.

Serves 3

LIGHTER, LEMONY BRAISED FENNEL

Follow the recipe for Silky Braised Fennel in Pink Sauce, but eliminate the vodka (keep the chicken broth amount the same), the tomato paste, and the heavy cream. Reduce the amount of salt to ¾ tsp. When chopping some of the fennel fronds, double the quantity—about 2 tsp total. When the fennel has finished braising and the broth is reduced, remove the pan from the heat and add 2 tsp fresh lemon juice and the chopped fennel fronds and stir well. Transfer to a serving dish.

Brown-Braised Baby Artichokes and Shallots with Pancetta

Believe it or not, baby artichokes don't take tons of time to prepare; you can trim nine of them in about 10 minutes. (They don't have the fuzzy choke in the middle, which needs to be removed in bigger artichokes.) Since they're now more available in grocery stores, I wanted to include this recipe so that you could learn the absolute best way to cook them—braising. I almost didn't because prepping and cooking does take 45 to 50 minutes total. But every time I make these, people devour them.

The dish has a complex and alluring flavor, because the artichokes and shallots are browned in pancetta drippings first, simmered in chicken stock, and finished with butter and lemon. You could probably eat these and nothing else for dinner (and some of my testers did). But they're also the perfect side dish for roast lamb—and, of course, roast chicken, roast beef, roast pork, and I don't know, maybe roast turkey, too! You can tell I like these.

2 WHOLE LEMONS, *halved*

9 BABY ARTICHOKES

3 TBSP UNSALTED BUTTER

1½ OZ/45 G THINLY SLICED PANCETTA, *chopped (about ⅓ cup)*

6 SMALL SHALLOTS, *halved and peeled*

½ TSP KOSHER SALT, *and more as needed*

1 CUP/240 ML LOW-SODIUM CHICKEN BROTH

1   *Set aside 1 lemon half for the sauce.* Squeeze and drop 2 of the remaining lemon halves into a medium bowl filled halfway with water. Cut the stems off the artichokes at the base. Peel away all of the outer leaves of each artichoke until you are left with a mostly lemon-limey-colored artichoke (it will be somewhat cone-shaped). The top third will still be a light green. With a sharp knife, cut about ¾ in/2 cm off each top, and cut the artichokes in half. With the remaining lemon half, rub the cut sides of the artichokes and drop the artichokes into the water.

2   *In a 10-in/25-cm straight-sided sauté pan* with a lid, melt 2 Tbsp of the butter over medium heat. Add the pancetta and cook, stirring, until crisp (about 5 minutes), turning the heat down to low if the drippings in the pan get too brown.

3   *Remove the pan from the heat* and transfer the pancetta with a slotted spoon to a paper-towel-lined plate. Arrange the artichoke halves (with whatever water still clings to them) and the shallot halves, cut side down, in one snug layer in the pan. Sprinkle with the ½ tsp salt.

4   *Return the pan to medium-high heat* and cook, without stirring, until the bottoms of the artichokes and the shallots are well browned, 6 to 7 minutes. (If the heat on your stove top is uneven, rotate the pan so that the bottoms get evenly browned.) Pour in the broth and cover the pan, leaving the lid slightly askew so that some steam escapes. Simmer gently, turning down the heat if necessary, until the broth is reduced to 1 or 2 Tbsp, 12 to 14 minutes. Uncover, add the remaining 1 Tbsp butter, and squeeze the reserved lemon half over all. Remove the pan from the heat, and stir, scraping up as much of the browned bits as possible. Taste for salt and immediately transfer to a serving platter. Sprinkle with the reserved pancetta.

Serves 3

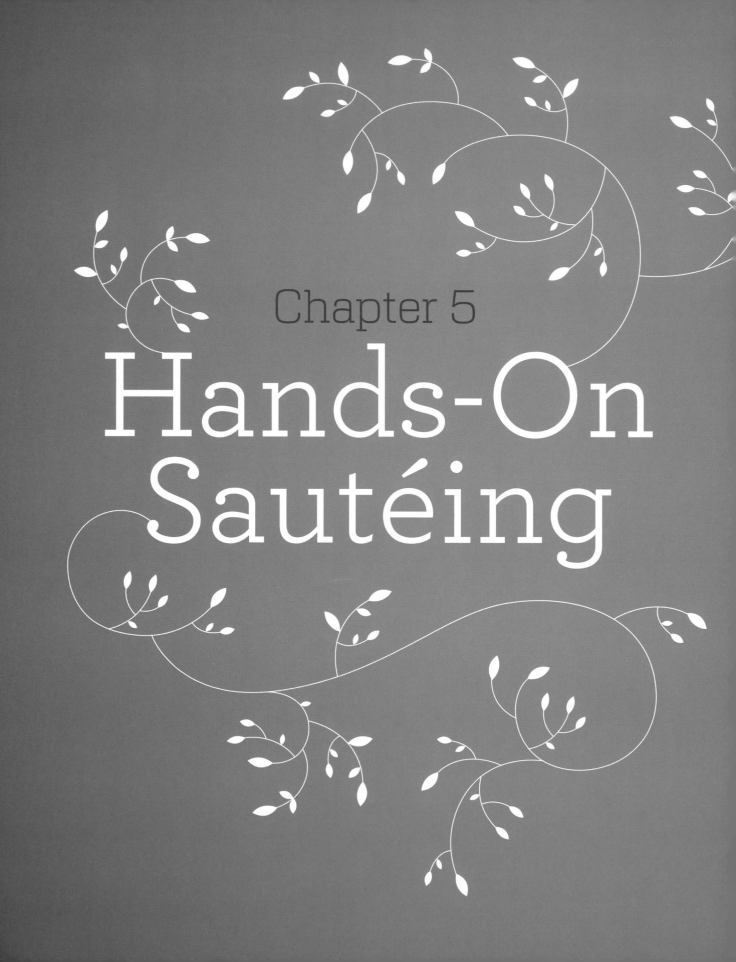

Chapter 5

Hands-On
Sautéing

METHOD: Hands on sautéing

EQUIPMENT: 10-in/25-cm straight-sided sauté pan, 12-in/30.5-cm nonstick skillet, heat-proof spatula, tongs

HEAT: The stove top, cranked up

....

Hands-On Sautéing: How It Works

Most likely you are in one of two camps about sautéing. Either you think it's a fancy French term for something that you can't imagine you would want to fuss with, or you think that it's something so simple that everyone knows how to do it. I'm sorry to have to tell you that if you're in either camp, you're wrong. Sautéing isn't difficult or laborious. But a good sauté—one that yields yummy vegetables—isn't a given, unless you follow a few simple tricks. And I mean simple.

Crank up the heat, and don't crowd the pan. If you did those two things, you'd be well on your way to nicely browned vegetables that still maintain some textural integrity. If your pan's not hot enough, you just won't get the browning that gives sautéed vegetables their characteristically yummy, caramelized flavor. And in most cases (though, after this, I'll give you a whole chapter of exceptions, just to confuse you), if the pan's too crowded, your vegetables will give off moisture and steam before they have a chance to brown. In fact, high-moisture vegetables like zucchini won't brown at all before breaking down completely if they are cooked in a crowded pan.

Next, we have to talk about fat (don't squirm): You don't want your vegetables to be swimming in fat, but you do need a little bit of this stuff to carry the heat and flavor around the pan. I like to sauté in olive oil, but I also like the flavor of butter. However, butter will burn over high heat because of its milk solids. A good compromise is a mix of both. You can get away with less fat in a nonstick pan; just remember that you will also get less of that browned stuff on the bottom of the pan. Sounds good, you think, right? Less cleanup. But that browned stuff has a ton of flavor in it and can often be reincorporated into the dish for more flavor. Whichever kind of pan you use, have a variety of hand tools nearby for stirring (tongs, heat-proof spatulas, wooden spoons). And keep in mind that *sauté* is from the French verb *sauter*, which means "to jump." This isn't an Olympic activity, but you will want to stay close by your pan and stir frequently. The really good news is that sautéing is quick; most of the recipes in this chapter come together easily in under 30 minutes.

For variety, I've included some recipes that are made in a nonstick skillet (a medium 10-in/25-cm size or a large 12-in/30.5-cm size) and others that require my truly favorite pan, the 10-in/25-cm straight-sided sauté pan. You don't have to spend a ton of money on a nonstick skillet with the latest hi-tech finish, but you do want something relatively hefty, with an aluminum base or core for good heat conductivity. If you want to splurge on something that will really last, you should check out Swiss Diamond skillets and the Anolon Advanced line of pans.

VEGETABLES FOR HANDS-ON SAUTÉING

VEGETABLE	WAY TO CUT	COOKING TIME
Asparagus	ends trimmed, cut on the diagonal into 1-in/2.5-cm pieces	10 minutes
Bell peppers	stemmed, seeded, cut into 1-in/2.5-cm pieces	12 to 14 minutes
Broccoli	1½- to 2-in-/3.75- to 5-cm-long florets, ¾ to 1 in/2 to 2.5 cm wide, with at least one flat side	7 to 9 minutes
Cabbage	very thinly sliced	8 minutes
Carrots	peeled, cut into ⅜-in-/9.5-mm-thick sticks or slices	10 to 12 minutes
Cauliflower	1½- to 2-in-/3.75- to 5-cm-long florets, ¾ to 1 in/2 to 2.5 cm wide, with at least one flat side	12 to 14 minutes
Collard Greens	very thinly sliced	1 minute
Corn kernels	cut from the cob	4 to 5 minutes
Eggplant	½-in/1.25-cm dice	12 to 14 minutes
Green beans	trimmed, cut on the diagonal into 1-in/2.5-cm pieces	6 to 8 minutes
Mushrooms, brown	quartered	10 to 12 minutes
Mushrooms, shiitake	stemmed and sliced	5 to 7 minutes
Parsnips	peeled, cut into ⅜-in-/9.5-mm-thick slices or sticks, or ½-in/1.25-cm dice	13 to 15 minutes
Snow peas	tails trimmed	3 to 5 minutes
Spinach	stemmed and washed	1 to 2 minutes
Sugar snap peas	tails and strings removed	6 to 7 minutes
Swiss chard	stemmed and washed	2 to 4 minutes
Zucchini	½-in/1.25-cm dice	7 to 9 minutes
Zucchini or summer squash	julienned	2 minutes

Foundation Recipe for Hands-On Sautéing

This is a very streamlined recipe, even more so than some of the other foundation recipes in this book. It's really just a starter kit to build on. Straightforward though this recipe is, don't miss the beauty here—hands-on sautéing is one of the quickest techniques in a cook's repertoire for preparing vegetables on a weeknight.

The other nice thing about a sauté is that it works with lots of different kinds of vegetables. For deeper flavor, I recommend including a little onion in your sauté, though I've made it optional in this recipe. I wouldn't use the onion with super-quick-cooking vegetables like collards or spinach unless you give it a head start, as it won't have enough time to soften up. On the other hand, when combining onions with longer-cooking vegetables, you should cut the onion into decent-size pieces (like 1-in/2.5-cm dice or ½-in-/1.25-cm-thick slices) so that it doesn't overcook before the other vegetables are done. As it browns, the onion will give off its magical flavor, which generally enhances anything. If onions aren't your thing, you could replace them with bell peppers, which work in a similarly aromatic way because of their high moisture content and bold flavor. You can also combine two or more vegetables in one sauté if their cooking times are similar.

1 TBSP EXTRA-VIRGIN OLIVE OIL

1 TBSP UNSALTED BUTTER

12 OZ TO 1 LB/340 TO 455 G YOUR CHOICE OF VEGETABLE *trimmed; see the table on page 81 for choices and how to cut them)*

1 SMALL YELLOW, RED, OR SWEET ONION *(2 to 3 oz/60 to 85 g), cut into slightly larger pieces than the vegetable (optional)*

¾ TSP KOSHER SALT

½ TO 1 TSP FRESH LEMON OR LIME JUICE

FRESHLY GROUND BLACK PEPPER

2 TSP FLAVORED BUTTER *(page 29; optional)*

1   *In a large (12-in/30.5-cm) nonstick skillet,* heat the olive oil and ½ Tbsp of the butter over medium heat. When the butter has melted, add the vegetable, the onion (if using), and the salt; toss well and raise the heat to medium-high. (If the pan seems crowded, turn up the heat to high.) Cook, stirring frequently, until the vegetables are softened and well browned, 2 to 15 minutes, depending on the vegetable (consult the table on page 81), or until wilted, 1 to 4 minutes, in the case of collard greens, spinach, and Swiss chard. Turn down the heat to low, add the remaining ½ Tbsp butter, and stir until melted. Sprinkle the lemon juice over all, stir again, season with pepper, stir, and serve. Alternatively, skip the ½ Tbsp butter and lemon juice and use 2 tsp of one of the flavored butters on page 29.

Serves 3 to 4

Corn Sauté with Chile and Lime

This is one of my favorite recipes in the book. Use this recipe as a template and feel free to make substitutions. Instead of cilantro, use mint or basil (or a combination); replace the lime zest with lemon; or try a combination of ground cumin and coriander in place of the ancho chile powder. You could also use a little diced bell pepper in place of some of the onion, or add ½ tsp of minced serrano pepper to the onions.

2 TBSP UNSALTED BUTTER

1 TBSP EXTRA-VIRGIN OLIVE OIL

1½ CUPS/165 G SMALL-DICED
YELLOW ONION *(1 medium-large onion),
preferably sweet*

1 TSP KOSHER SALT, *and more if needed*

2 SLIGHTLY HEAPING CUPS/315 G FRESH
CORN KERNELS *(from 4 medium ears; see tip
on page 67)*

⅓ TSP ANCHO CHILE POWDER

1 TSP FINELY GRATED LIME ZEST

FRESHLY GROUND BLACK PEPPER

¼ LIME

3 TBSP CHOPPED FRESH CILANTRO

1 *Melt 1 Tbsp of the butter* with the olive oil in a 10-in/25-cm sauté pan over medium-low heat. Add the onion and ½ tsp of the salt, cover, and cook, stirring occasionally, until translucent, about 5 minutes. Uncover, turn up the heat to medium, and sauté, stirring frequently, until lightly browned, 4 to 5 minutes more.

2 *Add the remaining 1 Tbsp butter,* the corn kernels, and the remaining ½ tsp salt. Cook, stirring frequently and scraping the bottom of the pan with a wooden spoon, until the corn is tender but still slightly toothy to the bite, 4 to 5 minutes. (It will begin to intensify in color, glisten, and be somewhat shrunken in size.) Add the chile powder and cook, stirring, for 1 minute. Stir in the lime zest and remove the pan from the heat. Let the corn sauté sit undisturbed for 2 minutes. Stir again, scraping up the browned bits from the bottom of the pan.

3 *Season the sauté* with a few generous grinds of pepper and a good squeeze of the lime. Stir in half of the cilantro. Let sit for another couple of minutes if you have time. Stir and season with more salt, pepper, or lime juice. Stir in the remaining cilantro just before serving.

Serves 4

Sautéed Shiitakes, Spinach, and Scallions

Sautéed shiitakes are so flavorful that they act like aromatics in this dish, lending the spinach their intensity. I sauté them in butter, not oil, because that buttery-mushroomy flavor and texture do great things with the silky spinach. A little touch of Asian seasonings—sesame oil and soy sauce—at the end means there's a slightly nutty and salty flavor, too. If you don't like Asian flavors, no worries. There is another, more straightforward spinach sauté in this chapter. Spinach is ultra-speedy to cook, making it a weeknight no-brainer. This dish, in fact, comes together in under 20 minutes; washing and spin-drying the spinach is the most time-consuming part.

This recipe feeds just two people (or one for an all veg-dinner), and would be just the thing with a couple of seared juicy rib-eyes.

2 TBSP UNSALTED BUTTER	**¼ TSP KOSHER SALT**
3½ OZ/100 G SHIITAKE MUSHROOMS, *stems removed, caps thinly sliced (about ¼ in/6.5 mm thick)*	**4 CUPS/115 G LIGHTLY PACKED STEMMED FRESH SPINACH LEAVES,** *washed and lightly dried*
⅓ CUP/21 G THICKLY SLICED *(about ½-in/1.25-cm)* **SCALLIONS** *(white and light green parts; about 4 medium)*	**1 TSP LOW-SODIUM SOY SAUCE**
	¼ TSP SESAME OIL

1   *In a medium (9- to 10-in/23- to 25-cm) nonstick skillet* over medium-low heat, melt the butter. Add the shiitakes and scallions and season with the salt. Toss and stir to coat with the butter. Cook, stirring occasionally, until the shiitakes are shrunken and very lightly browned, 5 to 7 minutes. (Don't brown too much, as shiitakes tend to toughen.) Add the spinach and the soy sauce and stir until all of the spinach is wilted, and it's well combined with the mushrooms, about 1 minute. Remove the pan from the heat, drizzle the sesame oil over the vegetables, stir, and serve.

Serves 2

Sautéed Sugar Snaps with Salami Crisps

This is, without a doubt, the easiest and quickest recipe in this book. The reason is that really good, really fresh sugar snap peas, with their sweet spring flavor and super-crunchy texture, need barely more than a turn in a hot sauté pan to be the perfect side dish. Yet there's a reason you often see peas with ham—all that sweetness benefits from a salty contrast. Salami is a fun and unexpected twist on this combination, since it's a slightly more flavorful cured pork product. It also gets delightfully crispy in the pan, as the peas brown and take on a deeper flavor, too. The payoff's big here for very little work.

This would be nice on one of those still-cold spring nights, served with creamy polenta snuggled up next to a piece of sear-roasted fish. Genoa salami is very flavorful and widely available (I like Applegate Farms); just make sure you buy it thinly sliced.

1 OZ/30 G VERY THINLY SLICED GENOA SALAMI	8 OZ/225 G SUGAR SNAP PEAS, *tails removed*
1 TSP EXTRA-VIRGIN OLIVE OIL	⅛ TSP KOSHER SALT

1   *Stack the salami slices* and cut them across into ¼-in/6.5-mm-wide strips. Pull the strips apart and spread them out in one layer on the cutting board (they're much easier to add to the pan when they're not clumped together).

2   *In a large (12-in/30.5-cm) nonstick skillet,* heat the olive oil over medium heat. When the oil is hot (it will loosen up and spread out), add the sugar snap peas and salt. Toss well. Cook, stirring occasionally, until the peas turn bright green, blister, and begin to turn a very light golden brown in spots, about 3 minutes. Add the salami strips and toss well.

3   *Continue to cook,* stirring occasionally, until the peas are browned in spots on both sides and the salami strips have shrunken, turned a darker brown color, and feel crisp, 3 to 4 minutes. (The salami will probably be crisp on the edges but still some-what pliable after 3 minutes. You can stop at that point if you don't want to cook the peas further, but I like the texture of the fully crisp salami, and the peas stay crisp even when cooked more.) Transfer to a serving platter or dinner plates.

Serves 3 to 4

Sautéed Carrots with Warm Olive and Mint Dressing

Carrots and olives were made to go together—I guess it's kind of a sweet and salty thing. Whatever it is, I love how it works in this gutsy sauté. Sometimes when I make this, I eat the whole thing myself. But if you'd like to share, serve the carrots with lamb chops rubbed with a Middle Eastern blend of spices like cumin, coriander, and cinnamon.

For this sauté, it's not necessary to fuss too much over the size of the carrot sticks. A little variation in size is no big deal. I usually wind up with a few extra-thin sticks that get a little bit blackened—and I love them.

By the way, I often make this recipe without the almonds. Either way, it's tasty; you could save the almonds for dressing this up a bit when you serve it to company.

2 TBSP EXTRA-VIRGIN OLIVE OIL

1 TSP RED-WINE VINEGAR

½ TSP DIJON MUSTARD

KOSHER SALT

1 LB/455 G CARROTS, *peeled cut into sticks ¼ to ⅜ in/6.5 to 9.5 mm thick and 2 to 3 in/ 5 to 7.5 cm long*

1 TSP MINCED FRESH GARLIC

2 TBSP FINELY CHOPPED PITTED KALAMATA OLIVES

2 TBSP CHOPPED FRESH MINT

2 TBSP COARSELY CHOPPED TOASTED ALMONDS *(optional; see tip on page 36)*

1   *In a small bowl,* combine 2 tsp of the olive oil, the red-wine vinegar, mustard, and a pinch of salt. Whisk until emulsified.

2   *In a large (12-in/30.5-cm) nonstick skillet,* heat the remaining 1 Tbsp plus 1 tsp olive oil over medium heat. When the oil is hot (it will loosen up), add the carrots and ½ tsp salt and toss well. Turn up the heat to medium-high and cook, stirring and tossing occasionally with tongs, until the carrots have lost their stiffness and are all nicely browned on at least one side (they will be a deep amber color with browning in spots), 10 to 12 minutes. (If they're browning too quickly, turn the heat down to medium.) Add the garlic, stir, and cook until fragrant and well combined, about 30 seconds. Remove the pan from the heat and carefully add the vinegar mixture (it will sputter), stirring immediately to distribute well. Add the olives and stir gently until well combined. Add half of the mint and stir again. Transfer to a serving platter or dinner plates and serve garnished with the remaining mint and the almonds, if desired.

Serves 3

Quick Collard Greens, Confetti-Style

My friend Randi tipped me off to this quick method for cooking collards. Up until then, I'd been braising them, which is a perfectly fine thing to do with these tough cookies. But how nice to be able to sauté them on a weeknight for a dish that cooks in just a couple of minutes and takes only about 25 minutes total, including trimming and washing the greens. The trick lies in how you cut the collards. If you roll the leaves up tightly like a cigar and slice them across very thinly (the French call this *chiffonade*), you will have something that looks like angel hair—or maybe linguine. Then all the collards need is a quick sauté with garlic and red pepper flakes to make a delicious side. I like to finish them with either Parmigiano-Reggiano or a touch of honey and vinegar.

Collards are such a great source of vitamin C, beta-carotene, calcium, and folic acid that you'll definitely be happy to add this recipe to your repertoire. It serves two but can easily be doubled to serve four (you'll only need 3 Tbsp of olive oil). Greens are always good with pork, but these collards would be a tasty weeknight side dish for just about anything. Sometimes I eat them with scrambled eggs on a meatless night.

½ LARGE BUNCH COLLARD GREENS	½ TSP KOSHER SALT
2 TBSP EXTRA-VIRGIN OLIVE OIL	½ TSP SHERRY VINEGAR *(optional)*
1 TSP MINCED FRESH GARLIC	½ TSP HONEY *(optional)*
BIG PINCH OF CRUSHED RED PEPPER FLAKES	6 TO 8 CURLS PARMIGIANO-REGGIANO *(optional)*

1   *Remove the stems* from the collard leaves by holding a stem with one hand and pulling the leaves away from it with the other. Rip the leaves completely in half lengthwise. You should have about 4 oz/115 g of trimmed collards. Rinse the leaves and dry them well. Stack them up on top of each other, roll them up tightly cigar-style, and, using a very sharp knife, slice them across into very thin ribbons (about ⅛ in/3.25 mm wide).

2   *In a large (12-in/30.5 cm) nonstick skillet,* heat the olive oil over medium heat. Add the garlic and cook until softened, fragrant, and just on the verge of turning brown, about 1 minute. Add the red pepper flakes, stir, and add the sliced greens and the salt. Cook, stirring to incorporate everything in the pan, until the greens turn bright green (at first) and then a darker green and are somewhat wilted, about 1 minute (don't cook much longer or they will begin to toughen). Remove the pan from the heat and taste. If you like, combine the sherry vinegar and honey in a small bowl, mix it well, and mix it into the greens. Transfer to a serving dish or dinner plates. Alternatively, skip the honey-vinegar mixture and serve the greens garnished with a few Parmigiano curls.

Serves 2

Sautéed Savoy Cabbage with Apple Cider Butter

In its simplest form, sautéed cabbage is a brilliant thing—the kiss of heat transforms this lowly vegetable, giving it a nutty flavor and a pleasant crisp-tender texture. This is why I've kept this recipe simple; I really didn't want to mess with the cabbage flavor much. (It's so very different from the boiled cabbage you might disdain). But I made two additions—a little sautéed onion and a finish of reduced apple cider (plus a bit of butter!), which don't complicate things too much. I've also added just a tiny bit of vinegar, because cabbage always benefits from an acid boost.

You'll recognize savoy cabbage by its wrinkly leaves—the outer ones are dark green. I prefer its texture to regular green cabbage. After cutting out the core, slice the leaves lengthwise to get the longest pieces.

½ CUP/120 ML APPLE CIDER

1½ TBSP UNSALTED BUTTER

¼ TSP RICE VINEGAR

1 TBSP EXTRA-VIRGIN OLIVE OIL

½ LARGE YELLOW ONION (4 to 5 oz/115 to 140 g), *thinly sliced*

KOSHER SALT

8 OZ/225 G THINLY SLICED SAVOY CABBAGE (*from about ½ head, cored*)

1 *In a small saucepan,* bring the apple cider to a boil. Let the cider cook (checking frequently) until it reduces to a syrupy consistency (1½ to 2 Tbsp), about 8 minutes. Do not over-reduce. Remove the pan from the heat and add ½ Tbsp of the butter. Swirl the pan until the butter has melted. Add the rice vinegar, stir well, and set aside.

2 *Combine the remaining 1 Tbsp butter* and the olive oil in a 10-in/25-cm straight-sided sauté pan over high heat (medium-high if your burners are powerful). When the butter has melted, add the onion and a pinch of salt and sauté, stirring, until the onion is softened and just beginning to brown, 2 to 3 minutes. Add all of the cabbage and ½ tsp salt and stir well. Cook, stirring occasionally, until the cabbage is limp and nicely browned and the bottom of the pan is very brown, about 6 minutes. Remove the pan from the heat and let the cabbage sit for a minute or two. The moisture it gives off will help loosen the browned bits on the bottom of the pan. Briefly and gently reheat the cider butter to loosen it. Drizzle it over the cabbage, scraping it all out of the pan with a silicone spatula. Stir and thoroughly combine the cider butter with the cabbage, scraping up any remaining browned bits. Transfer the vegetables to a serving dish.

Serves 3

Sautéed Asparagus with Pancetta and Parmigiano for Two

I know it doesn't make sense, but brown is actually a good color when it comes to sautéed green vegetables—especially asparagus, which takes on a wonderful nutty flavor when caramelized in a sauté pan. A little bit of pancetta adds extra depth to this quick sauté.

For this recipe, I prefer to use asparagus that are slightly thick. Cutting them on the diagonal makes them look very pretty. When you're shopping for asparagus, look for tight heads and take a whiff of the bunch. If it's starting to go bad (which is common in the grocery store, unfortunately), it will smell off and feel slimy. If you have access to fresh local asparagus during the spring, don't pass it by. It's a vegetable treat that is worth a detour. If you want to serve four people with this dish, use a large (12-in/30.5-cm) nonstick skillet and double everything exactly.

8 MEDIUM-LARGE ASPARAGUS SPEARS, *ends trimmed or snapped away (6 to 7 oz/ 170 to 200 g trimmed)*

1 TSP EXTRA-VIRGIN OLIVE OIL

1 TBSP UNSALTED BUTTER

2 THIN SLICES PANCETTA (*about ½ oz/ 15 g total), coarsely chopped (roughly ½-in/1.25-cm pieces)*

SCANT ¼ TSP KOSHER SALT

½ TSP BALSAMIC VINEGAR

1 TBSP FINELY GRATED PARMIGIANO-REGGIANO

1 *Slice the asparagus* on a very sharp angle into pieces that are about 2 in/5 cm long and about ¼ in/6.5 mm in diameter at their thickest point. You'll get 6 to 7 pieces from each stalk.

2 *In a medium (9- to 10-in/23- to 25-cm) nonstick skillet,* heat the olive oil and ½ Tbsp of the butter over medium-low heat. When the butter has melted, add the pancetta and cook until crisp, 3 to 5 minutes. Remove the pan from the heat and transfer the pancetta with a slotted spoon to a paper towel–lined plate. Add the asparagus to the skillet, season with the salt, and return the pan to the heat, raising it to medium-high. Cook, stirring frequently, until all of the asparagus pieces are nicely browned, up to 10 minutes. They will still be firm, but not crunchy. Remove the pan from the heat and add the remaining ½ Tbsp butter and the balsamic vinegar (it will sizzle). Stir right away and keep stirring until the butter has melted. Transfer the asparagus to a serving dish or dinner plates and garnish with the Parmigiano and the pancetta crisps.

Serves 2

Brown Butter Summer Squash "Linguine"

Hoorah! There's finally a great way to cook summer squash, that poor unfortunate victim of too many "vegetable medleys," in which the overgrown squash is thickly sliced, overcooked, and served in a pool of liquid. Young squash—diced small and cooked fast—are yummy. Even better, if you treat yourself to a really cool hand tool—a julienne peeler, which only costs about seven dollars—you can make the quickest, tastiest squash dish ever.

To make squash "linguine," peel the squash all the way around until you reach the seed core. The teeth on the peeler cut the squash into thin strips, which not only look beautiful, but cook in a heartbeat. I like to make the longest strips possible by peeling the entire length of squash in one stroke. However, to avoid running the peeler into your fingers, you can do one end of the squash first, flip the squash around, and then peel the other. Your strips will be half as long, but still nice looking.

In this recipe, I quickly sauté the "linguine" in brown butter for a super-fast side dish. You could just wrap it up with salt and a squeeze of lemon, but I've added almonds, as nutty flavors pair really well with all squashes. (Hazelnuts are good here, too.) You can substitute zucchini for half of the summer squash, if you like. Serve this with grilled scallops or shrimp.

1½ LB/680 G YOUNG YELLOW *(summer)* SQUASH *(about 4)*	1 TSP KOSHER SALT
2 TBSP UNSALTED BUTTER	2 TSP CHOPPED FRESH TARRAGON OR PARSLEY
2 TBSP FINELY CHOPPED ALMONDS OR HAZELNUTS	½ LEMON

1 *Wash and dry the squash* and trim off the ends. Using a julienne peeler, peel the squash lengthwise all the way around, dropping the strips into a bowl. Continue peeling until you reach the seed core. Discard the core and peel the other squash in the same fashion. Toss the squash strips and separate any that are clumping together.

2 *In a 10-in/25-cm straight-sided sauté pan,* melt the butter over medium-low heat. Add the almonds and swirl the butter around in the pan. Cook the butter until it reaches a nutty brown color (the almonds should be light brown by then), about 2 minutes. The color turns quickly so keep an eye on it—it will be more flavorful if you take it beyond a very light brown, but you don't want it to turn black. Immediately add the squash and salt. Toss the squash gently with tongs until it is well coated with the butter. Continue cooking just until the squash becomes slightly limp, about 1 minute. Remove the pan from the heat, stir in half of the chopped herbs, and squeeze a little of the lemon over the squash and toss. Taste and add more lemon, if desired. Transfer the squash to a serving dish or plates and garnish with the remaining herbs.

Serves 3 to 4

Spinach with Shallots and Parmigiano

Sometimes I prepare sautéed spinach simply with slivers of garlic and a few red pepper flakes. Perfectly delicious but the truth is this slightly richer version, with a bit of cream and Parmigiano, is my favorite. I like the sweet, earthy flavor the sautéed shallots add, too. You could even think of this as a much lighter version of creamed spinach. This spinach would be my top pick for a fast, delicious sidekick to a sautéed chicken breast. The recipe also works well with Swiss chard.

I'm a big fan of fresh spinach (by fresh I mean bunches of leaves on the stem, rather than bagged spinach). I actually enjoy the sort of Zen-like process of stemming and washing the pretty clusters of leaves, but it does make a simple dish more time-consuming than it has to be. You can certainly do this with bagged baby spinach; just look for the bags with larger leaves, which have more body and flavor. If you do buy fresh, you can stem, wash, and dry the spinach a day ahead and keep it in a paper towel–lined zip-top bag.

1 TBSP EXTRA-VIRGIN OLIVE OIL

2 SMALL SHALLOTS, *thinly sliced (about 1½ oz/45 g)*

KOSHER SALT

1 BUNCH FRESH SPINACH (*10 to 12 oz/ 285 to 340 g*) OR 5 TO 6 OZ/140 TO 170 G BABY SPINACH LEAVES, *washed and dried*

1 TSP HEAVY CREAM

1 TBSP FINELY GRATED PARMIGIANO-REGGIANO

1   *Heat the olive oil* in a medium (9- to 10-in/23- to 25-cm) nonstick skillet over medium-low heat. When the oil is hot (it will loosen up), add the shallots and a pinch of salt and stir with a silicone spatula to distribute them in the oil. Cook, stirring, until the shallots are softened and just a light golden brown, about 4 minutes. (Don't brown too much or the shallots will taste slightly bitter.)

2   *Add half of the spinach* and another pinch of salt and stir and fold the spinach with tongs until most of it is wilted and dark green, 1 to 2 minutes. Add the remaining spinach and stir well again until the spinach is almost completely wilted, another minute or two. Remove the pan from the heat, add the cream, and stir to incorporate. Add the Parmigiano, stir well, and serve right away.

Serves 2

Mahogany Mushrooms

Who doesn't love sautéed mushrooms? That is, of course, if they're cooked properly. I have a few tricks to help you pull this off. First, I start with brown cremini mushrooms, which I think have a meatier texture than white button mushrooms. Then I quarter or halve them (rather than slice) so they maintain their appealing heft. I cook the mushrooms on pretty high heat, until—and this is most important—all the moisture they give off during the sauté has evaporated. (Don't worry if the pan looks dry at first; the mushrooms give off moisture as they cook.) I look for an appealing orangey-brown color (the tasty stuff) to know they're done.

These sautéed mushrooms, come with an easy sauce. Actually, it's more like a glaze, and it adds not only a lot of flavor, but a nice sheen, too. Use them in a warm spinach salad, as a topping for a sirloin steak, or even as part of an antipasto selection.

1 TBSP SOY SAUCE	2 TBSP EXTRA-VIRGIN OLIVE OIL
1 TBSP FRESH LEMON JUICE	1 LB/455 G CREMINI (baby bella) MUSHROOMS, quartered if large, halved if small
2 TSP DARK BROWN SUGAR	
2 TSP KETCHUP	¾ TSP KOSHER SALT
½ TSP WORCESTERSHIRE SAUCE	2 TSP MINCED FRESH GARLIC
2 TBSP UNSALTED BUTTER	FRESHLY GROUND BLACK PEPPER

1   *In a small bowl,* whisk together the soy sauce, lemon juice, brown sugar, ketchup, Worcestershire sauce, and 1 Tbsp of water and set the bowl near the stove. Put a shallow serving dish near the stove as well.

2   *In a 10-in/25-cm straight-sided sauté pan,* heat 1 Tbsp of the butter with the olive oil over medium-high heat. When the butter has melted, add the mushrooms and salt, stir right away, and continue stirring until the mushrooms have absorbed all of the fat.

3   *Let the mushrooms sit* and cook for 2 minutes, then stir once. Don't worry; the pan may look crowded and dry, but keep the heat up at medium-high. Let it sit and cook, stirring infrequently (they will squeak when you stir them), until the mushrooms are shrunken, glistening, and some parts have developed a deep orange-brown color, about 10 minutes (the bottom of the pan will be brown).

4   *Turn the heat down to low,* and add the garlic and remaining 1 Tbsp butter. Stir and cook until the butter is melted and the garlic is fragrant, about 30 seconds. Whisk the soy sauce mixture again and very carefully add it to the pan. You'll need to scrape out the brown sugar, but don't stand directly over the pan as there will be sputtering. Stir and cook just until the liquid thickens slightly and coats the mushrooms, 15 to 20 seconds more. Season with a few grinds of pepper and quickly transfer the mushrooms and all of the sauce to a serving dish.

Serves 4

Chapter 6
Walk-Away Sautéing

METHOD: Walk-away sautéing

EQUIPMENT: 10-in/25-cm straight-sided sauté pan, heat-proof spatula, tongs, wooden spoon, liquid measure

HEAT: The stove top—not too hot

Walk-Away Sautéing: How It Works

Something pretty cool is going to happen to you if you cook from this chapter. You will learn (or improve your ability) to cook using all of your senses—sight, smell, touch, taste, even hearing. This is kind of scary and exciting at the same time, because what I'm really saying is that this method is not an exact science. But that's actually a good thing in terms of flavor, because the transformation these vegetables undergo during cooking is nothing short of magic.

Here's the big picture: You'll start with hearty vegetables (like carrots or Brussels sprouts) and cut them into even (usually medium-size) pieces. You'll combine them with some aromatics—like mushrooms, garlic, or onions—and cook them slowly in a decent amount of olive oil in a sauté pan until they're tender and deeply golden. Often a bit of pancetta or bacon and some fresh herb sprigs go in the pan, too. The pan will look quite crowded, but that's intentional. The vegetables will help each other cook by giving off some of their own steam. (That's why this method is great for low-moisture vegetables and not so great for things like zucchini, which would get mushy cooked this way.)

The finer point is this: There is an ideal amount of heat and time to both brown the vegetables slowly and cook them through. It's a slow, gentle heat (usually what's labeled "medium" on my stove, but it could be "medium-low" on yours). With a generous amount of olive oil, the vegetables will usually be perfectly cooked in 25 to 30 minutes. You may have to do a little fiddling around—adjusting your heat or adding a little more olive oil—when first trying these recipes on your stove and with your pan.

Usually the vegetables don't brown at all in the first several minutes of cooking (at least they shouldn't!). They will release their moisture (you will hear a gentle sizzle), and you'll only have to stir them occasionally (you can *walk away*). About halfway through cooking, the vegetables will begin to brown (and sizzle a little more loudly). Sometimes, though, if the heat is initially too high or there isn't enough olive oil, browning can happen more quickly, before your vegetables have had a chance to start getting tender. The solution here is to simply turn the heat down—the browning will slow down, giving the vegetables more time to become tender.

Also, depending on the vegetable mix, sometimes the pan can get dry. A little more olive oil and a little lower heat is the solution here. One thing not to worry about: The bottom of the pan will almost always get quite brown. This happens with all of the sautés as the vegetables are in the pan for so long that some of their proteins and sugars begin to stick to the pan. In some recipes, I call for washing up a little of this to make a bit of sauce. But when there is an especially large amount of browning on the bottom of the pan, some of it will have become bitter, so I don't go crazy scraping it up. Don't freak out, no matter how much buildup there is; if you're using a good, heavy stainless-steel pan, it will wash right off with soap and hot water.

I first learned this method from the late chef Leslie Revsin (who was the first female chef at the Waldorf-Astoria in New York years ago). In her post-restaurant career, she wrote lots of articles for us at *Fine Cooking* magazine, but none more enlightening than one on a cooking method she called slow-sautéing. Leslie liked to use a cast-iron pan for her recipes, and I often use mine when I'm improvising on a weeknight. But for this book, I developed the recipes using a heavy-duty, straight-sided stainless-steel sauté pan, which more folks are likely to own (especially after reading this book!).

For most of these recipes, I like to stir with a heat-proof silicone spatula (as opposed to my tongs, which some people have alleged are surgically attached to me). These veggies want to be babied—gently stirred. In turn, they will reward you with lots of good flavor.

In this chapter, you might find that starting with one of the recipes in the list on page 97 is the best way to learn this technique. (I recommend the green bean recipe—it's very straightforward and tastes good even if it's slightly under- or overcooked.) Then you can go back to the foundation recipe any night you like and improvise your own combination. But either way, I think you'll find this unusual method delivers very satisfying results.

Foundation Recipe for Walk-Away Sautéing

One pan, some chopping, a little stirring. Then it's time to sip a glass of wine or open the mail. The beauty of this technique is its manageability, especially once you've done these recipes a few times. As I said in the introduction to this chapter (please read it before tackling this recipe), at first you may need to do a little finessing—turning the heat down if the veggies are browning too fast, maybe adding a little more olive oil if the pan seems dry. So I've limited the variety of vegetables in this foundation recipe to make things easier. Unlike other foundation recipes in the book, this one does not have a table of vegetables with lots of choices. Your choices are limited to those in the ingredients list, but they are varied enough to make some really yummy combinations possible.

You'll want to pick one hearty vegetable (say, cauliflower), combine it with an aromatic vegetable (say, cremini mushrooms), and add some pork (say, pancetta) if you like. You can also put a few fresh herb sprigs into the mix. (If you don't use pork, include the herb sprigs for sure.) For finishing the dish, I've given you a small amount of liquid (chicken broth), acid (juice or wine), and butter to introduce a little bit of moisture. As I have noted elsewhere, I like to cut broccoli and cauliflower florets in half so that the cut side can lie flat in the pan and brown better. Other vegetables in this recipe should be cut for maximum browning surface, too. Don't slice vegetables too thinly or they will break down before they're properly browned.

In this recipe, the bottom of the pan will often get very brown toward the end of cooking. Starchy vegetables like parsnips, in particular, will leave lots of browned bits. Do not worry about this. You can add some more olive oil if the vegetables need moisture, but otherwise continue to cook until the vegetables are browned and tender.

Please be sure you're cooking in a heavy-duty 10-in/25-cm straight-sided sauté pan. (A slope-sided skillet of about the same size will work all right, too, though because of its openness it doesn't allow quite as much steaming to occur.) And use all of the olive oil the first few times you make this recipe. Some vegetable combinations will work all right with just 3 tablespoons, but others will brown or dry out too quickly.

1 TBSP LOW-SODIUM CHICKEN BROTH

2 TSP FRESH LEMON OR LIME JUICE, SHERRY, WINE, OR OTHER SPIRITS

1 LB/455 G HEARTY VEGETABLES (*Brussels sprouts, broccoli, cauliflower, turnips, carrots, or parsnips*)

6 OZ/170 G AROMATIC VEGETABLES (*red, yellow, or sweet onion; fennel; large shallots; brown mushrooms such as cremini, a.k.a. baby bella*)

¼ CUP/60 ML EXTRA-VIRGIN OLIVE OIL, *and more if necessary*

2 OZ/60 G THINLY SLICED HAM, THINLY SLICED PANCETTA, OR BACON, *cut into 1-in/2.5-cm pieces (optional)*

3 TO 5 SPRIGS FRESH THYME, ROSEMARY, OR SAGE (*optional*)

¾ TO 1 TSP KOSHER SALT

½ TBSP UNSALTED BUTTER

2 TBSP CHOPPED TOASTED PINE NUTS, HAZELNUTS, ALMONDS, PECANS, OR WALNUTS (*optional; see tip on page 36*)

1 *In a small bowl,* combine the broth and lemon juice and set aside.

2 *Cut your vegetables* into similarly sized pieces. Broccoli and cauliflower should be cut into florets about 1½ in/3.75 cm long and 1 in/2.5 cm wide (cut through the middle of each large floret). Turnips should be cut into wedges about 1 in/2.5 cm long and ¾ in/2 cm wide. Cut carrots and parsnips slightly on the diagonal into coins or half-moons. At the thinner end of carrots or parsnips, cut oval shapes on a sharp diagonal about ¾ in/2 cm thick. At the thicker end, cut the vegetable in half lengthwise first, and then slice into half-moon-shaped pieces about ½ in/1.25 cm thick. Cut onions and fennel into large dice or into pieces with ¾- to 1-in/2- to 2.5-cm sides. Quarter large shallots and medium mushrooms; cut larger mushrooms into six pieces. You should have 12 to 14 oz/340 to 400 g vegetables after trimming.

3 *In a 10-in/25-cm straight-sided sauté pan,* heat the ¼ cup/60 ml olive oil over medium heat. When the oil is hot (it will shimmer and loosen), add the hearty and aromatic vegetables, the ham (if using), the herb sprigs (if using), and the salt, (¾ tsp if using bacon or pancetta). Use tongs to toss everything thoroughly and to coat with the oil. Reduce the heat to medium-low or whatever seems moderate on your stove. You should hear a gentle sizzling.

4 *Cook, stirring with a silicone spatula,* only occasionally at first, but more frequently as the vegetables (and the pan) begin to brown, gently sliding the spatula under the vegetables and loosening a little of the browned bits when possible. Continue cooking until the vegetables are all well browned and tender (check with a paring knife or the tines of a fork), between 20 and 35 minutes, depending on the vegetables, the heat, and the pan. The bottom of the pan will be very brown, depending on the vegetables. When done, broccoli and cauliflower will remain somewhat firm; they don't need to be completely limp, but they should be somewhat pliable. (If they aren't, add a little more olive oil and continue to cook for a few more minutes.) All other vegetables should feel fairly tender when poked with a paring knife or the tines of a fork.

5 *Remove the herb sprigs* (if used), reduce the heat to low, and add the liquid and butter to the pan. Stir gently, dislodging whatever browned bits are fairly loose, but not going crazy, until the butter has melted and the liquid is reduced, about 30 seconds. Remove the pan from the heat, transfer the vegetables to a serving platter, and garnish with the toasted nuts, if desired.

Serves 4 to 5

Gingery Sweet Potato and Apple Sauté with Toasted Almonds

I like using the walk-away sauté technique for sweet potatoes because they get tender and nicely browned without losing their shape. Apples are a natural match, of course, but since they cook a bit more quickly, I add them later. Handle the apples and the sweet potatoes gently; just by using a heat-proof silicone spatula to stir rather than tongs. As you're cooking, don't worry if the pan seems to brown more than the vegetables; that will happen. Just keep stirring and cooking, turning the heat down a bit if necessary, until the sweet potatoes are all tender when pierced with a paring knife.

For pizzazz, I've spiked this with plenty of ginger and topped it with crunchy toasted almonds. Try serving this in a warm salad with hearty greens and sliced pork tenderloin.

1 TSP CIDER VINEGAR

2 TSP LOW-SODIUM CHICKEN BROTH

1½ TBSP UNSALTED BUTTER

2 TBSP EXTRA-VIRGIN OLIVE OIL

1½ MEDIUM SWEET POTATOES, unpeeled (12 to 13 oz/340 to 370 g), cut into ½-in/1.25-cm dice (about 2¾ cups)

1 SMALL YELLOW ONION (about 4 oz/ 115 g), cut into ½-in/1.25-cm dice

1 TSP KOSHER SALT

1 GOLDEN DELICIOUS APPLE (6 to 7 oz/ 170 to 200 g), unpeeled, cored and cut into ½-in/1.25-cm dice or pieces

2 TSP FINELY CHOPPED FRESH GINGER

2 TSP CHOPPED FRESH PARSLEY

2 TBSP ROUGHLY CHOPPED TOASTED SLICED ALMONDS (see tip on page 36)

1 *Combine the cider vinegar* and broth in a small bowl and set aside.

2 *In a 10-in/25-cm straight-sided sauté pan,* melt 1 Tbsp of the butter with 1 Tbsp of the olive oil over medium heat. Add the sweet potatoes, onion, and salt. Turn the heat down to medium-low. (The pan should still sizzle; if your stove is less powerful, you can stay on medium and lower the heat later if needed.) Cook, stirring occasionally, until the onion is softened and lightly browned and the sweet potatoes have turned bright orange and are starting to brown, 10 to 12 minutes. (The bottom of the pan will be lightly browned, and the sweet potatoes will have started to soften.)

3 *Add the remaining* 1 Tbsp olive oil and the apple. Turn the heat down just a tiny bit more and continue to cook, stirring frequently, until the sweet potatoes are tender (test with a paring knife) and the apple and the onion are browned, 8 to 12 minutes.

4 *Add the ginger* and stir to incorporate. Remove the pan from the heat, clear a small spot in the pan, and add the vinegar-broth mixture (it will sizzle) and the remaining ½ Tbsp butter. Stir well immediately to incorporate the butter and any browned bits loosened from the bottom of the pan (most will remain). Add the parsley, stir, and transfer to a serving platter or plates. Garnish with the toasted almonds.

Serves 4

Dark and Crispy Pan-Fried Red Potatoes

When I was developing recipes for this book, I kept testing this one over and over again to get it right. At least that's what I told myself I was doing. The truth is, I just love these potatoes so much that I'd think of any excuse to make them. You could eat them just as easily for breakfast with eggs as you could for dinner with steak or chicken. If you want to serve these with something more delicate, like a sear-roasted fish fillet, you can leave out the rosemary.

There are two tricks for this version of classic pan-fried potatoes. First, don't move the potatoes around at all for the first several minutes; you want to let a nice brown crust form. Then, after the potatoes start browning on several sides, keep cooking them until they're a very dark caramel brown. It may seem scary, but this is the secret to extra-crispy potatoes—just keep going. When I asked friends to cross-test this recipe, the browning time varied a bit with everyone's stoves and pans. So keep an eye on the color to help determine when the potatoes are done. If you've got a cast-iron skillet, use it to make these potatoes. Be sure to cut your potatoes into ½-inch dice.

3 TBSP EXTRA-VIRGIN OLIVE OIL

1 LB/455 G RED POTATOES, *unpeeled, cut into ½-in/1.25-cm dice or pieces*

1 TSP KOSHER SALT, *and more if needed*

1 TBSP UNSALTED BUTTER

½ TSP MINCED FRESH GARLIC, *or more if you like*

½ TSP CHOPPED FRESH ROSEMARY

COARSE SEA SALT *(optional)*

1 *In a 10-in/25-cm straight-sided sauté pan* or a seasoned cast-iron skillet, heat the olive oil over medium heat. When the oil is hot (it will loosen and spread out), add the potatoes, immediately spreading them out in one layer. Sprinkle with the 1 tsp kosher salt. Cook, without stirring or moving, until the potatoes have developed a nice crust on the bottom and can be moved, 7 to 9 minutes (check with a thin metal spatula). Flip over all of the potatoes with the spatula and cook for 4 to 5 minutes more without stirring.

2 *Continue to cook,* now flipping and scraping more often, until the potatoes are a deep caramel brown color on most sides and feel tender when pierced with the edge of the spatula, 12 to 15 minutes. (If necessary, lower the heat a bit toward the end of cooking.) Turn the heat down to low and add the butter, garlic, and rosemary. Stir until the butter is melted and the garlic is softened, 30 seconds to 1 minute. Transfer to a serving dish and season with more kosher salt or coarse sea salt (if using).

Serves 3

Sautéed Broccoli with Mellow Garlic and Thyme

This is definitely the recipe to convert broccoli-bashers, since the method of slow-sautéing yields a crisp floret and lots of caramelized flavor. (If you already like broccoli, you'll love this.) I could eat this for supper with a bowl of creamy polenta or smashed red potatoes—no big honking protein needed!

Like the other sautés in this chapter, once you get this going, you can tend to other things. However, you will want to check in from time to time, not only to stir but also to see how fast the broccoli is browning. At first, the broccoli will turn bright green, and then it will slowly begin to brown and get tender. The trick is to keep the heat about right so that the browning and tenderizing (for lack of a better word) happen at about the same rate. If the broccoli (or the pan) seems to be browning too quickly, turn the heat down a bit; and if the pan looks very dry, add a little more olive oil. (Remember, it's good for you.)

¼ CUP/60 ML EXTRA-VIRGIN OLIVE OIL, *and more if needed*

2 OZ/60 G THINLY SLICED PANCETTA *(about 6 slices), each cut into quarters*

10 LARGE GARLIC CLOVES, *halved lengthwise*

12 TO 14 OZ/340 TO 400 G BROCCOLI FLORETS, *each 2 in/5 cm long with one flat side (6 to 7 cups)*

¾ TSP KOSHER SALT, *and more if needed*

6 SPRIGS FRESH THYME

1 *In a 10-in/25-cm straight-sided sauté pan,* heat the ¼ cup/60 ml olive oil over medium heat. Add the pancetta pieces in one layer and cook until they just start to bubble and shrink, about 1 minute. Add the garlic and cook, without stirring, until the bottoms are just starting to turn a light golden brown, 2 to 3 minutes. Add the broccoli, ¾ tsp salt, and thyme sprigs, and stir well to coat the broccoli.

2 *Reduce the heat* to low (or at the lowest end of medium-low) and cook, stirring only occasionally, until the broccoli is browned (the floret end will be darker and crispy) and the garlic is browned and tender, 20 to 25 minutes. (If the pan looks very dry, add a little more olive oil and turn the heat down just a bit.) The broccoli will be cooked through but the stems will still have a somewhat crisp texture. Taste and season with a little more salt, if desired. Remove the pan from the heat, discard the thyme sprigs, and transfer the vegetables to a serving dish or dinner plates.

Serves 4

Caramelized Green Beans and Sweet Onions

When I was the editor of *Fine Cooking* magazine, my staff used to kid me that my favorite color was brown. That's because I always complained at tastings that things (bread crumbs, chickens, roasted vegetables—you name it) were never browned enough. In cooking, complex flavors develop when certain chemical reactions occur, and browning—whether caramelizing or toasting—is one of those great opportunities for flavor development. If you love caramelized onions, you already know this.

It just so happens that the sweet onions and the beans will caramelize in about the same amount of time, so they're a perfect pair. In fact, this recipe takes so little prep that it's one of the faster ones in this chapter (about 30 minutes in all). Don't skimp on the time, though; you want the beans and onions to be really well browned (and tender) for the best flavor. They won't look pretty, but they will taste delicious.

Everyone will love these, so serve them with something comforting like meat loaf and mashed potatoes or crispy oven-fried chicken. The sage adds subtle flavoring here, so feel free to add more leaves if you like.

8 TO 10 OZ/225 TO 285 G SWEET ONION *(such as Vidalia or Walla Walla; 1 small or ¾ medium)*

3 TBSP EXTRA-VIRGIN OLIVE OIL, *and more if needed*

12 OZ/340 G GREEN BEANS, *trimmed and halved*

16 TO 20 MEDIUM FRESH SAGE LEAVES, *plus 4 sprigs for garnish (optional)*

¾ TSP KOSHER SALT, *and more if needed*

2 TBSP FRESH ORANGE JUICE

1 *Cut the onion in half* lengthwise, trim the ends, and peel it. Cut each half lengthwise into ½-in-/1.25-cm-wide slices, angling your knife toward the center of the onion with each cut (a radial cut). Discard any very thin or small pieces of onion. In a 10-in/25-cm straight-sided sauté pan, heat the 3 Tbsp olive oil over medium heat. Add the onion, green beans, sage leaves, and ¾ tsp salt. Using tongs, stir and flip the vegetables to coat them well with the olive oil. Reduce the heat to medium-low.

2 *Cook, stirring and tossing* the vegetables with tongs only occasionally at first, but more frequently as browning begins, until the vegetables are very well browned and tender, 20 to 24 minutes. The bottom of the pan will be very brown, too. (As you're stirring, brush the vegetables back and forth over the browned spots on the bottom of the pan—the onion will release juices, which help release the browned bits.) Remove the pan from the heat, add the orange juice, and stir vigorously with a wooden spoon to scrape up the browned bits from the bottom of the pan. Taste and season with more salt if necessary. Transfer the vegetables to a serving dish or dinner plates, and garnish with the sage sprigs, if you like.

Serves 4

Sautéed Turnips with Ham and Molasses

Yes, I actually put chopped peanuts on this, too. Sorry, you might have to be Southern to understand how this classic trio—ham, molasses, and peanuts—could work so well with something as quirky as turnips. But trust me, even if you live in Manitoba, you will like how well these flavors work with the slightly piney taste of this root vegetable. (And you can always substitute another nut.) This recipe takes 45 minutes to make.

2 TSP MOLASSES

1 TBSP PLUS 1 TSP LOW-SODIUM CHICKEN BROTH

1 LB/455 G SMALL PURPLE-TOPPED TURNIPS, *unpeeled*

¼ CUP/60 ML EXTRA-VIRGIN OLIVE OIL

1 MEDIUM RED ONION (*about 7 oz/200 g*), *cut into ¾-in/2-cm dice*

½ TSP KOSHER SALT

3 OZ/85 G THINLY SLICED HONEY HAM, *roughly chopped (about ⅓ cup)*

½ TBSP UNSALTED BUTTER

¼ CUP/45 G ROUGHLY CHOPPED UNSALTED PEANUTS

1. *Whisk together the molasses* and the broth in a small bowl. Trim the ends off the turnips and set them down on one of the cut sides on a cutting board. If the turnips are taller than 1½ in/3.75 cm, cut them in half crosswise (through the equator). Leave the smaller ones in one piece. Then, as if cutting a pie, cut each turnip or turnip half into 8 to 10 equal wedges. (The wedges shouldn't be thicker than ¾ in/2 cm at the widest end.)

2. *In a 10-in/25-cm straight-sided sauté pan,* heat the olive oil over medium heat. Add the turnips, onion, and salt. Stir to coat. Cook, stirring only occasionally at first and more frequently as the vegetables begin to brown, until the turnips are nicely browned and mostly tender (the onion will also be browned), 25 to 27 minutes.

3. *Turn the heat down* to medium-low, add the ham (the pan will sizzle), and continue to cook, stirring, until the ham gets a bit browned and slightly shrunken, and all the turnips feel tender (pierce with a paring knife or fork), 5 to 7 minutes more. (The turnips will turn from a whitish to a yellowish color when cooked through.) Don't worry if some of the onion seems very dark.

4. *Add the molasses-broth mixture* and the butter, remove the pan from the heat, and stir until the butter is melted, scraping to incorporate any browned bits from the bottom of the pan. Let the vegetables sit for a few minutes, and stir and scrape again. Transfer them to a serving platter and garnish with the peanuts.

Serves 4

Southwestern Butternut Squash Sauté

The combination of flavors and textures in this sauté makes it one of my favorites in this chapter. I love crunchy pepitas (Mexican pumpkin seeds), cool cilantro, and warm spices like cumin, coriander, and smoky chipotle chile pepper. The very slow sautéing softens the texture and intensifies the flavor of a popular fall vegetable, butternut squash.

2 TBSP EXTRA-VIRGIN OLIVE OIL

1 LB/455 G PEELED AND SEEDED BUTTERNUT SQUASH, *cut into ½-in/1.25-cm dice (about 4 cups)*

1 MEDIUM-LARGE YELLOW ONION *(about 6 oz/170 g), cut into ½-in/1.25-cm dice*

1 TSP KOSHER SALT

1 TBSP UNSALTED BUTTER

¼ TSP GROUND CORIANDER

¼ TSP GROUND CUMIN

⅛ TSP CHIPOTLE CHILE POWDER

2 TSP PURE MAPLE SYRUP

1 TSP FRESH LIME JUICE

2 TBSP CHOPPED FRESH CILANTRO

1 OZ/30 G CRUMBLED FRESH GOAT CHEESE *(optional)*

2 TBSP TOASTED PEPITAS *(Mexican pumpkin seeds; see tip on page 36)*

1 | *In a large (12-in/30.5-cm) nonstick skillet,* heat the olive oil over medium heat. Add the squash, onion, and ¾ tsp of the salt. Toss thoroughly to coat. Cook, stirring with a silicone spatula only occasionally at first, and then more frequently as the vegetables brown, until the squash is tender and lightly browned and the onion is well browned, 20 to 22 minutes. Remove the pan from the heat.

2 | *In a small saucepan,* melt the butter over very low heat. Add the coriander, cumin, chile powder, and the remaining ¼ tsp salt, and cook, stirring, for a minute or two to soften the spices. Add the maple syrup, simmer for 15 to 30 seconds, and remove from the heat. Stir in the lime juice.

3 | *Drizzle the butter mixture* over the squash and stir thoroughly but gently with a silicone spatula to incorporate. Add the cilantro and fold it in gently. Transfer the squash to a small serving platter and sprinkle with the goat cheese (if using) and the pepitas. Let sit for a few minutes for the goat cheese to soften a bit and for the flavors to marry. Serve warm.

Serves 4

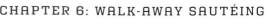

Smoky Spanish Carrots and Fennel with Toasted Hazelnuts

This one's not for the vegetable wimp. During a slow sauté, carrots and fennel both gently caramelize and take on deep, earthy flavors. A bit of smoked Spanish paprika (pimentón) deepens the allure, and toasted hazelnuts add more intrigue. This would be the perfect side for the classic Spanish chicken and rice dish *arroz con pollo*.

It does take time—about 30 minutes—to get the carrots and fennel to the perfect texture. But like most of the walk away sautés, there's not a heck of a lot you have to do during that time. Stir. Sip wine. Stir. Sip wine. That's all. Oh, and you can fret a little when you think the pan is getting too brown. But it really isn't a problem, I promise. Keep cooking until the carrots have shrunk in size quite a bit and are lightly browned all over (some pieces will be very brown). Test both the carrots and fennel with a paring knife to see if they're done. If they still feel a little firm, just keep sautéing for a few more minutes.

To speed this along a bit, prep the carrots and fennel, get them cooking, then do the rest of the prep, including toasting the hazelnuts.

¼ CUP EXTRA-VIRGIN OLIVE OIL	1 TSP KOSHER SALT
1 LB/455 G CARROTS, *peeled, trimmed, and cut into ¾-in/2-cm coins at the thin end and ½-inch/1.25-cm half-moons at the thick end*	1 TBSP SHERRY OR RICE WINE
	½ TSP SPANISH SMOKED PAPRIKA *(pimentón de la vera)*
1 SMALL FENNEL BULB, *trimmed, cored, and cut into ¾-in/2-cm pieces (yielding 10 to 12 oz/285 to 340 g)*	3 TBSP COARSELY CHOPPED TOASTED HAZELNUTS, *(see tip on page 36)*

1   *In a 10-in/25-cm straight-sided sauté pan,* heat the olive oil over medium heat. Add the carrots and fennel and season with the salt. Stir well with a silicone spatula to combine. Continue to cook, stirring occasionally at first, and more frequently as the pan begins to brown. Be patient, as it will not look like much is happening in the beginning. Keep stirring and cooking (and don't worry about the pan browning), until the carrots have shrunken quite a bit, are tender (test with a paring knife) and somewhat browned, and the fennel is tender, 28 to 30 minutes.

2   *Add the sherry to the pan* and stir well until it has almost evaporated. Sprinkle the paprika over the vegetables and stir for just a few seconds to incorporate the spice and release its flavor. Remove the pan from the heat and let cool for a minute. Transfer to a serving dish and garnish with the toasted hazelnuts.

Serves 3 to 4

Bacon and Rosemary Sautéed Brussels Sprouts and Baby Bellas

This is the kind of dish Brussels sprouts were born to star in—earthy, rustic, and deeply flavored (gotta love those mushrooms). It's just a wonderful example of how magical the transformation can be when you use this walk-away sautéing method. Please be adventurous and try this if you've never really been a fan of Brussels sprouts, as I do think you'll change your mind.

Brussels sprouts vary in size from teeny-tiny to huge mini-cabbage hefties. In fact, I had one that weighed 0.2 oz/5 g and one that weighed 1.2 oz/35 g in the same batch. So to make sure they'll all cook evenly, follow the prep instructions in the recipe.

Once the ingredients for this recipe are prepped, everything goes into the pan at the same time; then all you have to do is stir occasionally and be bold about cooking the vegetables until they are nicely browned. The result is a side dish that could really be a meal in itself with a bit of brown rice—or the perfect thing with roast chicken or pot roast some Sunday night.

1 LB/455 G BRUSSELS SPROUTS	**2 SPRIGS FRESH ROSEMARY,** *each about 4 in/10 cm long*
8 OZ/225 G CREMINI *(baby bella)* **MUSHROOMS,** *wiped clean*	**1 TSP KOSHER SALT**
¼ CUP/60 ML EXTRA-VIRGIN OLIVE OIL	**2 TBSP UNSALTED BUTTER,** *cut into pieces*
2 OZ/60 G BACON, *cut into 1-in/2.5-cm pieces*	**¼ LEMON**

1 *Trim the stem ends* of the Brussels sprouts. Cut the smallest sprouts into quarters. Cut the largest sprouts in half, and then cut each half into thirds. In both cases, cut lengthwise through the stem so that a piece of the core holds the leaves together. Cut the mushrooms in a similar fashion: Quarter the smallest ones, and cut the larger ones in half and then into thirds, lengthwise.

2 *In a 10-in/25-cm straight-sided sauté pan,* heat the olive oil over medium heat. Add the sprouts, mushrooms, bacon, and rosemary. Season with the salt and, using tongs, stir well to combine everything. The pan will be very crowded; that's okay.

3 *Turn the heat down* to medium-low and cook, stirring occasionally at first and more frequently when the vegetables begin to brown, until the vegetables are well browned and the Brussels sprouts are tender (the stems may still be a bit firm), 28 to 30 minutes. (I like to use a metal spatula for turning the vegetables toward the end of cooking.) The bottom of the pan will be quite brown. Remove the pan from the heat, discard the rosemary, and add the butter pieces. Stir gently with a silicone spatula until all of the butter has melted. Give a generous squeeze of lemon over all and stir again. Taste and season with more lemon, if needed. Serve warm.

Serves 5

Chapter 7

Two-Stepping

METHOD: Two-stepping (boil first, then sauce or sauté)

EQUIPMENT: Large, wide pot (4- to 5-qt/3.8- to 4.7-L capacity) or a large saucepan (about 3 qt/3 L); a sauté pan or small saucepan; colander; tongs; dish towels

HEAT: The stove top—high for boiling, low for saucing

....

Two-Stepping: How It Works

What in the world, you're wondering, is two-stepping? Sounds like an old-fashioned ballroom dance, doesn't it? Well it is a little bit old-fashioned, because it involves boiling vegetables. I hate to use that word—boiling—because everyone cringes with bad memories of overcooked vegetables. But it wouldn't be accurate to say that we're just blanching or even parboiling the vegetables in this chapter, as we're actually boiling them until they're tender—but *only* until tender. Then we're treating them to a turn in the sauté pan, the saucepan, or the salad bowl to add flavor.

For many vegetables—especially tough leafy greens—boiling is really the quickest, easiest, and most reliable way to get consistently good results. Also, by boiling greens first, you can drain off the excess liquid they shed during cooking before you sauce them in a variety of different ways. In this chapter, for instance, I've made a warm maple-pancetta pan sauce for Tuscan kale, a creamy ginger and garlic sauce for mustard greens, and a Spanish-flavored mix of chorizo, honey, and smoked paprika for kale—three very different palettes for three greens.

This method is also perfect for delicate spring vegetables like fresh peas, fava beans, and fiddlehead ferns, which tend to get overcooked (or improperly cooked) with other cooking methods. Two-stepping is also a great way to cook dense vegetables, like potatoes, that you intend to use in salads. And it's the absolute best way to achieve perfectly cooked (not undercooked!) green beans.

You'd think boiling would be pretty straightforward, but it's the timing that is tricky. All of my recipes have been cross-tested on a variety of stoves and pots, but that doesn't mean that the timing will be the same for you. How fast water returns to a boil after vegetables are dropped in depends on the power of your burners and the material of your pot. Also, different batches of the same kind of vegetable cook at different rates, depending on their age and size. So pretend you're a chef-in-training and learn to taste for doneness. You'll get to know the subtle differences in toughness and tenderness. For instance, greens like kale and mustard have a distinctly rubbery texture when undercooked. There's a window of a few minutes when they begin to soften up before they start overcooking, and that's when you want to nab them.

For boiling, I like to use a wide, shallow pot, called a Dutch oven. It does not have to be made of cast iron. Any 4- to 5-qt/3.8- to 4.7-L pot that's wider than it is tall will do. If you don't own a pot like this and plan to buy one, don't skimp (get a heavy, thick-bottomed pot). This is the pot you'll use to make small batches of stews and braises. A large, wide pot like this is usually ideal for boiling vegetables, because it allows plenty of room for water to surround the vegetables and cook them evenly. However, in some of these recipes, a pot with a smaller capacity (a 3-qt/3-L saucepan) will provide enough room.

You will also notice that I often let vegetables cool on dish towels. I think this is a gentle way of letting them steam off a little excess moisture, and they still stay relatively warm for two-stepping. You can arrange a few layers of dish towels right on your counter, or you can put the dish towels on top of a sheet pan that can be carried to the stove.

I hope I'm not making this sound more complicated than it is. Because aside from the fact that you might have to get a colander or an extra pan out for this method, the recipes are relatively quick and very rewarding in flavor. Plus, often the boiling can be done ahead if you have the opportunity, so all you have to do is sauce at the end.

If you're looking for something simple, start with the foundation recipe, which is based on a chart of cooking times and ideal cuts for some popular vegetables. I've given you a couple of quick ways to flavor them, but you can also steal one of the sauces from another recipe in this chapter or another part of the book. Keep in mind that I'm using the word "sauces" loosely. One sauce could be as simple as a drizzle of infused oil; another could be a more complex sauté of aromatics.

VEGETABLES FOR TWO-STEPPING

VEGETABLE	WAY TO CUT	BOILING TIME
Asparagus	1-in/2.5-cm pieces cut on the diagonal	3 to 4 minutes
Broccoli crowns	1½-in-/3.75-cm-long florets, halved	3 to 4 minutes
Carrots	⅜-in/9.5-mm half-moon slices	6 to 8 minutes
Dandelion greens	trimmed and cut into 3-in/7.5-cm lengths	3 to 4 minutes
Fava beans	removed from pod	2 to 3 minutes before peeling
Green beans or yellow wax beans	ends trimmed	4 to 8 minutes
Kale	ribs removed, leaves torn into pieces	5 to 7 minutes
Mustard greens	ribs removed, leaves torn into pieces	6 minutes
Peas, fresh	shelled	2 to 3 minutes
Potatoes, red or gold	cut into 1-in/2.5-cm pieces	10 to 14 minutes (start in cold water)
Snow peas	tails and strings removed	1 minute
Sugar snap peas	tails and strings removed	2 minutes
Tuscan kale	ribs removed, leaves torn into pieces	4 to 6 minutes

Foundation Recipe for Two-Stepping

To become comfortable and efficient using this technique, get in the habit of setting up the two-step process before you do anything else. Put a large pot of water on one burner on the stove, and a medium skillet on another. Put a few layers of dish towels on a work surface near the stove or on a sheet pan. Put a colander in the sink if you'll be cooking leafy stuff or potatoes. Then you can get the water started while you prep the veggies. And while the vegetable cooks, you can make your simple flavor "boost" in a skillet.

Because the foundation recipe is meant to be a simple guide to a technique, I've kept the options for finishing very simple (these include a choice between butter and olive oil). You can easily dive right into one of the other recipes in the chapter if you'd like something racier. (Or you can use one of the Flavored Butters on page 29.) By now you must have read that fat acts as a transporter of valuable nutrients (not to mention flavor), so don't be tempted to skip it altogether.

KOSHER SALT

12 TO 18 OZ/340 TO 515 G YOUR CHOICE OF VEGETABLE (*10 to 12 oz/ 285 to 340 g trimmed; see the table on page 116 for choices and how to cut them*)

2 TBSP UNSALTED BUTTER OR EXTRA-VIRGIN OLIVE OIL

1 TSP MINCED FRESH GARLIC OR GINGER (*optional*)

1 TSP FRESH LEMON OR LIME JUICE, *and more if needed*

2 TSP FINELY CHOPPED FRESH PARSLEY, CHIVES, MINT, THYME, OR CILANTRO (*optional*)

1 *Fill a wide 4- to 5-qt/3.8- to 4.7-L pot* two-thirds full of water and add 2 tsp kosher salt. Bring the water to a boil and add the vegetable. (Potatoes are the exception here; start them in cold water.) Begin timing immediately (don't wait for the water to return to a boil). Consult the table on page 116 for approximate cooking times, and then begin checking a minute or two before the vegetable should be done. Bite into a piece to check for tenderness (or poke potatoes with a paring knife); continue cooking and tasting just until tender.

2 *If cooking leafy greens* or potatoes, drain them well in a colander. For all other vegetables, use tongs to transfer the vegetable directly to dish towels to let some of the excess moisture evaporate. Squeeze as much water as possible out of the greens (you may need to run cool water over them briefly to be able to handle them)

3 *Meanwhile,* in a medium (9- to 10-in/23- to 25-cm) nonstick skillet, heat the butter over medium heat.

If using butter: Heat the butter just until it has melted, add the garlic (if using) and cook until it is softened and fragrant, 1 to 2 minutes. (If not using the garlic, cook the butter until it turns a nutty brown color, 3 to 4 minutes [watch carefully]. Remove the skillet from the heat and add the 1 tsp lemon juice to it.

If using olive oil: Heat the olive oil until it loosens and spreads out. Add the garlic (if using) and cook until it is softened and fragrant, 1 to 2 minutes. Remove the skillet from the heat and add the 1 tsp lemon juice.

4 *Add the cooked vegetable* to the skillet. If using leafy greens, first give them one more squeeze before transferring them to the skillet. Season with ¼ to ½ tsp salt, and thoroughly stir all together. Add the fresh herbs (if using), stir, and toss again, and taste. Add more lemon juice or salt, if desired, and serve.

Serves 3 to 4

Provençal Green Beans with Lemon-Pepper Oil and Herbed Sea Salt

My friend Ruth Lively, who's a terrific gardener and cook, tipped me off to dressing green beans while they're still warm with nothing but a really flavorful extra-virgin olive oil and a generous sprinkling of coarse sea salt. The fragrant olive oil mixing with the warmth of the beans creates a flavor that's just naturally delicious. Notching the flavor up just a bit isn't a bad idea either, so I often use an infused oil and an herb salt to dress the beans. The Provençal combination I'm including here is a lemon-pepper oil and an herb salt that you can make with either lavender or rosemary.

I have a lot of lavender growing in my yard, and it's taken me a while to figure out how to use it in the kitchen. I've found that just a little bit combined with a good sea salt, like fleur de sel, makes an intriguing condiment, not just for green beans, but also for other vegetables and grilled meats. That said, I certainly understand if it sounds too floral for you—opt for rosemary or just plain sea salt, but don't be shy about the amount of salt you use. The lemon-pepper oil is really versatile; drizzle any extra on grilled fish or grilled bread. (Make some extra and keep it in the fridge.)

You will have to taste the green beans after a few minutes of cooking to get a sense of how firm they are—that way when you taste again in another minute, you'll feel the difference. Keep cooking the beans just until you can easily bite through them (you won't feel resistance). I assure you that they'll still be green. You don't want to overcook them, but undercooked beans have a slightly unpleasant, rubbery texture to them. How fast your beans cook will depend in part on how old and how big they are; you can remove thinner ones sooner than the rest.

Serve these beans in high summer with mustardy grilled chicken. Or just eat them with your fingers after dressing them.

2 TSP KOSHER SALT

1 LB/455 G GREEN BEANS, *stem ends trimmed*

2 TBSP QUICK-INFUSED LEMON-PEPPER OIL *(recipe follows) or best-quality extra-virgin olive oil*

½ TO 1 TSP PROVENÇAL HERB SALT *(recipe follows) or coarse sea salt, preferably fleur de sel*

{ Continued }

1. *Fill a large saucepan* half full with water, add the salt, and bring to a boil. Arrange a few layers of dish towels on a work surface to drain the beans. Add the beans to the boiling water and begin timing immediately. Boil until the beans are tender to the bite but still green, 5 to 8 minutes. (Begin tasting after 4 minutes; the cooking time will vary, depending on the age of the beans and how quickly your stove top returns water to a boil.) Don't undercook, as toothy green beans are not the goal here. Drain the beans, or use tongs to lift them out of the water, and spread them out on the towels to let excess moisture drain and evaporate, about 5 minutes.

2. *Transfer the beans* to a shallow serving dish and drizzle most of the oil over them. Sprinkle with some of the herb salt. Toss gently and add more oil to coat well and more herb salt. Taste a bean and add still more salt if you like (be generous!). Serve warm.

Serves 4

QUICK-INFUSED LEMON-PEPPER OIL

This oil keeps well in the fridge, so double or triple the amounts if you like and use it on grilled fish or any steamed vegetable.

| 2 TBSP EXTRA-VIRGIN OLIVE OIL | | 8 COARSE GRINDS BLACK PEPPER |
| 1 TBSP PACKED GRATED LEMON ZEST | | |

1. *Pour the olive oil* into a small bowl and add the lemon zest and pepper. Let sit for 15 to 20 minutes before using.

Yields 2 tablespoons

PROVENÇAL HERB SALT

This salt delivers a lot of flavor. Lavender can be overpowering, though, so take care not to include more than ¼ tsp of chopped buds per ½ tsp of salt. Mix this not too long before using. This salt is delicious on roast lamb, as well as on warm green beans.

¼ TSP CHOPPED FRESH LAVENDER BUDS OR ROSEMARY LEAVES   ½ TSP SEA SALT

1. *In a small bowl,* combine the lavender with the salt and mix well with your fingers. Let sit for a few minutes before using.

Yields ¾ teaspoon

Peas with Lemon, Mint, and Scallions

A funny thing happened when I sent out this recipe to some folks for cross-testing. Everyone came back and said they loved it, but that they had tried it with frozen peas after trying it with fresh, and had better results! This was because the "fresh" peas they got from the market were large, old, and starchy. Unfortunately, fresh peas should not really be available year-round at the grocery store, as they don't store well. We should all enjoy them in late spring and early summer when we see them at the farmers' market, or we should grow our own, because they're sweet, tender, and delicious. If you do see fresh peas at the grocery store, they will definitely be fresher if they are still in the shell. The rest of the year, you shouldn't think twice about using frozen peas. And this is just the recipe to dress them up and give them a bright flavor.

These peas are the perfect Easter side dish; serve with roast leg of lamb and buttered new potatoes. Or for weeknights, serve with seared lamb rib chops and a simple rice pilaf. If you don't have scallions, you can use an equal amount of minced shallots. You can also substitute chives for the mint. And I've included a variation made with a little bit of coconut milk. Those would still be good with lamb, preferably grilled kebabs.

If you're entertaining, you can boil the fresh peas or thaw the frozen peas ahead of time. It will take less than 10 minutes to finish them on the stove top at dinnertime.

KOSHER SALT

8 OZ/225 G SHELLED FRESH PEAS (about 2 cups) or frozen peas (about 1½ cups)

2 TBSP UNSALTED BUTTER

4 LARGE SCALLIONS (white and light green parts), thinly sliced

¼ CUP/60 ML HEAVY CREAM

2 TBSP FINELY CHOPPED FRESH MINT

½ TSP PACKED FINELY GRATED LEMON ZEST

FRESHLY GROUND BLACK PEPPER

{ Continued }

1   *If using fresh peas:* Fill a large saucepan half full with water and 2 tsp salt and bring to a boil. Drop the peas into the boiling water and cook until just tender (taste one or two), 2 minutes for smaller peas, 3 minutes for larger, older peas. Begin timing immediately; don't wait for the water to return to a boil. Use a mesh strainer to transfer the peas to a dish towel or a few layers of paper towels to drain. Discard the water the peas were boiled in, but reserve the pot.

    If using frozen peas: Put the peas in a colander and run cold water over them for a few minutes until they're mostly thawed. Spread them out on a few layers of dish towels to drain.

2   *Melt the butter* in the reserved saucepan over low heat. Add the scallions and sauté until softened, about 3 minutes. Add the heavy cream, half of the mint, the lemon zest, ¼ tsp salt, and a few grinds of pepper. Bring the mixture to a boil and cook until it thickens slightly and a wooden spoon leaves a wide path when scraped across the bottom of the pan, about 1 minute. Add the peas and stir until they're heated through and well coated with the sauce, 1 minute more. Remove the pan from the heat, taste for salt and pepper, and serve immediately, garnished with the remaining mint.

Serves 3

FRESH PEAS WITH LIME AND COCONUT MILK

To give the peas a slightly tropical twist, replace half of the heavy cream with coconut milk (canned, well stirred), replace the lemon zest with lime zest, and replace the mint with cilantro. When adding the cream-coconut mixture to the sautéed scallions, simply bring it to a boil and immediately add the peas. You won't need to let the cream reduce.

Crushed Red Potatoes with Scallions, Pancetta, and Sour Cream

These potatoes are like the really good stuff inside your favorite baked potato. Not quite mashed, a little more than crushed, and a bit like a hash—I thought I might call them crashed, but they're much more delicious than that sounds. They're inspired by the fried potatoes my mom used to make a lot when we were growing up; she always boiled them first. But the second step in this recipe is not so much frying as it browning, and with the scallions and pancetta mixed in, it does feel a bit like hash. And it tastes oh so yummy. Be sure to use a nonstick pan for the browning step to prevent sticking.

What to eat these with? Anything. Everything. You decide. If you have any leftovers (which is unlikely), shape them into patties and fry them up for breakfast (see the variation following). If you like, you can substitute shallots for the scallions, and Greek-style yogurt for the sour cream. It's all good.

1 LB/455 G SMALL RED POTATOES, *cut into 1-in/2.5-cm pieces*

2¼ TSP KOSHER SALT

2 TBSP UNSALTED BUTTER

1½ OZ/45 G VERY THINLY SLICED PANCETTA *(about 5 slices)*

⅓ CUP/20 G SLICED SCALLIONS *(white and light green parts)*, PLUS 1 TBSP THICKLY SLICED SCALLIONS *(dark green part only)*

FRESHLY GROUND BLACK PEPPER

3 TBSP SOUR CREAM

1   *Put the potatoes* in a large saucepan with 2 tsp of the salt and cover with cold water by about 1 in/2.5 cm. Cover the pot, bring the water to a boil, and adjust the heat for a gentle simmer. Cook until the potatoes are tender when pierced with a paring knife, 10 to 14 minutes (check after 10 minutes, because the time will vary with the freshness of the potatoes). Drain the potatoes and return them to the pot. Let sit for 5 minutes to evaporate excess moisture (they can sit for up to 30 minutes).

2   *In a medium (9- to 10-in/23- to 25-cm) nonstick skillet,* melt the butter over medium-low heat. Add the pancetta slices and cook, flipping occasionally, until browned and crisp, 5 to 7 minutes. Transfer the pancetta to a paper-towel-lined plate. Turn the heat down to low and add the ⅓ cup/20 g scallions. Cook, stirring, until the scallions are softened and lightly browned, about 1 minute. Add the potatoes to the pan, season with the remaining ¼ tsp salt, and toss them gently with the scallion butter. Return the heat to medium-low and arrange the potatoes with one cut side down. Cook, without stirring, until the bottoms are just lightly browned, 5 to 6 minutes.

3   *With a hand masher,* begin to crush and mash the potatoes, incorporating the scallions and butter as you go. When the potato pieces are about the size of large marbles (don't mash completely, though some will lump together), remove the pan from the heat, season the potatoes with a few grinds of pepper, and add the sour cream. Continue mashing and folding just until most of the sour cream is incorporated (you'll still see some sour cream). Do not mash too much, as you want the potatoes to have lots of texture. (And don't worry about the skins falling off and catching on the masher—just return them to the potatoes; remember this is sort of like baked potatoes!) Transfer the potatoes to a serving dish or dinner plates. Crumble the pancetta slices over the potatoes and garnish with the thickly sliced scallion greens.

Serves 3

CRUSHED POTATO PATTIES

To fry leftover crushed potatoes, take them out of the fridge 15 or 20 minutes ahead of time to take off the chill. Scoop a small amount of potatoes with your hands and shape into patties that are about ¾ in/2 cm thick and 2 in/5 cm in diameter. Melt 1 tsp of butter with 1 Tbsp of olive oil in a small nonstick skillet over medium-low heat and add 2 or 3 patties. Cook until browned on one side, 4 to 5 minutes. Flip and brown the other side. Serve right away.

Brown-Butter Asparagus with Pine Nuts

This is certainly a handy dish to have in your repertoire, because the asparagus can be boiled ahead and finished later in minutes. Unlike traditional poached asparagus, the spears in this recipe are cut into pieces and dropped into boiling water. They only take 3 to 4 minutes to cook.

Step two in this recipe is making a little brown butter in a saucepan. While the butter is browning, so are the pine nuts, so all that's left is a squeeze of lemon. (If you've never made the deliciously nutty-tasting indulgence known as brown butter, you're in for a treat.)

You could double this recipe if you wanted to serve it as a side dish for an Easter dinner of ham or roast leg of lamb. But this would also be perfectly delicious with salmon or chicken. Be sure to cut the pieces on the diagonal, as they look quite elegant this way.

2½ TSP KOSHER SALT

1 BUNCH ASPARAGUS, *ends trimmed, cut on a diagonal into 2-in-/5-cm-long, sharply angled pieces (yielding 11 to 12 oz/310 to 340 g)*

2 TBSP UNSALTED BUTTER

⅓ CUP/45 G PINE NUTS

½ TO 1 TSP FRESH LEMON JUICE

FRESHLY GROUND BLACK PEPPER

1 *Arrange a few layers* of dish towels on a work surface to drain the asparagus. Fill a large (3-qt/3-L) saucepan half full with water and add 2 tsp of the salt. Bring to a boil and drop in the asparagus pieces. Begin timing immediately (don't wait for the water to come back to a boil). Cook the asparagus until crisp-tender, 3 to 4 minutes. Don't overcook; they'll cook a bit more as they cool and again when mixed with the brown butter.

2 *Drain the asparagus* in a colander and spread them on the dish towels to let excess water evaporate. Return the saucepan to the stove and melt the butter over low heat. Add the pine nuts and ¼ tsp salt, turn the heat up to medium, and cook, stirring constantly, until the butter turns a nutty brown color and the pine nuts turn mostly golden, 3 to 4 minutes. (Keep an eye on the butter, as it turns color quickly. If it becomes dark brown, that's fine. If it blackens, you'll have to start over.)

3 *Remove the pan from the heat* so that the butter doesn't continue to cook and add the asparagus and the remaining ¼ tsp salt. Toss to combine thoroughly, sprinkle with ½ tsp of the lemon juice, and toss again. Taste and add a little more lemon juice if you like. Season with freshly ground pepper. Serve warm.

Serves 3 to 4

Spicy Mustard Greens with Ginger-Garlic Cream

Mustard greens are always spicy—in a hot, pungent, peppery kind of way. So I sometimes like to tame that heat with a cooling dash of cream, though I infuse the cream first with a good hit of garlic and ginger. This is easy and quick, with little chopping—just some smashing to break up the fibers of the ginger "coins" (and get your frustrations out, too).

Like most of the greens in this chapter, the mustard greens are boiled first, because this allows you to cook them perfectly and drain them well. Don't undercook them, or the greens will be tough. If you'd like to use a different green (or vegetable) with this sauce, you certainly can. Just refer to the table on page 116 for the boiling time.

Sausages—that's what comes to mind to serve with the greens. Buy some of the good-quality organic sausages that are in the markets now. Split them in half and fry or grill them. Nestle them in a shallow bowl with the greens, and you've got a simple supper.

KOSHER SALT	2 LARGE GARLIC CLOVES, *smashed*
1 LB/455 G MUSTARD GREENS	4 SLICES FRESH GINGER (¼-in/6.5-mm-thick coins), *smashed (see tip)*
½ CUP/120 ML HEAVY CREAM	

1   *Fill a wide 4- to 5-qt/3.8- to 4.7-L pot* three-quarters full of water. Add salt and bring to a boil. Meanwhile, remove the stems from the mustard greens. Grab the rib of a leaf with one hand and rip the two leafy sides away from it with the other hand. Rip the leaves into several smaller pieces. Add all of the leaves to the boiling water and stir to submerge them. Cook until the leaves are tender, about 6 minutes. (Begin tasting the leaves at about 4 minutes so that you'll be able to feel the difference when the greens become tender.)

2   *Drain the greens thoroughly* in a strainer and rinse them with cool water just until they are cool enough for you to handle. Squeeze as much water as possible out of the greens.

3   *In a small (2-qt/2-L) saucepan,* combine the cream, garlic, and ginger. Bring to a boil and reduce to a simmer. Cook until the cream has reduced by about half and has thickened (larger bubbles will begin to form in the cream and you will be able to see the bottom of the pan). Remove the pan from the heat and use a slotted spoon to remove most of the ginger and garlic pieces; it's okay if some are left behind. Add the mustard greens to the saucepan, put it back over medium-low heat, and stir to break up the greens and incorporate the cream with them. Cook just until warmed through—any longer and the greens will weep moisture. Taste and season with more salt if needed.

Serves 2 to 3

Tip: **To smash the ginger, arrange the coins on a cutting board underneath plastic wrap and whack them with a meat mallet until the fibers are mostly broken.**

Provençal Kale with Chorizo, Pimentón, and Honey

The flavors in this dish are really robust thanks to the chorizo, smoked paprika, and the combination of garlic, honey, and vinegar. It's a bit tricky to track down *pimentón de la Vera* (Spanish smoked paprika), but McCormick has it in their Gourmet Collection now, so it is in some grocery stores. And you can order it online from Penzeys.com.

2 TSP HONEY	**1 BUNCH KALE** (*14 to 15 oz/400 to 425 g*), *stems removed, leaves ripped into 2-in/5-cm pieces (yielding about 8 oz/225 g), washed*
1 TSP SHERRY VINEGAR	
¼ TSP SPANISH SMOKED PAPRIKA	**2 TBSP EXTRA-VIRGIN OLIVE OIL**
¼ TSP GROUND CUMIN	**2 OZ/60 G CHORIZO**, *cut into small dice (¼ to ⅜ in/6.5 to 9.5 mm)*
⅛ TSP GROUND CINNAMON	**2 TSP MINCED FRESH GARLIC**
2½ TSP KOSHER SALT	**1 TSP UNSALTED BUTTER**

1   *Whisk together the honey and sherry vinegar* in a small bowl. In another small bowl, combine the paprika, cumin, cinnamon, and ½ tsp of the salt. Set aside both bowls.

2   *Fill a wide 4- to 5-qt/3.8- to 4.7-L pot* three-quarters full with water, add the remaining 2 tsp salt, and bring to a boil. Add the kale to the boiling water and start timing immediately. Taste a leaf after 5 minutes. It shouldn't be tough or rubbery. If it is, cook for 1 to 2 minutes more. Drain the kale very thoroughly in a strainer in the sink. As the kale cools a bit, press down on it to force some of the excess liquid out.

3   *In a large (12-in/30.5-cm) nonstick skillet,* heat the olive oil over medium heat and add the chorizo. Cook until it's somewhat shrunken and a deeper red (it will have given off some fat), 4 to 5 minutes. Add the garlic and stir to soften, about 30 seconds. Turn the heat down to low. Push the chorizo to one side of the pan and add the butter to the cleared space. As the butter melts, sprinkle the reserved spices directly on top of it. Mix the butter and spices together (this will help the spices release their aroma) and then stir them into the chorizo and garlic. Remove the pan from the heat.

4   *Give the kale* one more squeeze to force out more liquid and then add it to the sauté pan. Working quickly, use tongs to stir and thoroughly incorporate the kale with the contents of the pan. Drizzle on the honey-vinegar mixture and toss and stir again to combine well. Transfer the kale and everything in the pan to a serving dish.

Serves 3

Tuscan Kale with Maple, Ginger, and Pancetta

Bacon, maple, and ginger may sound like a funny combination until you translate those flavors into salty, sweet, and spicy. Then you realize how well they work with the slightly bitter, earthy flavor of the beautiful crinkly kale known variously as Tuscan kale, *cavalo nero*, dinosaur kale, black kale, and Lacinato kale. I love greens, but I find that many people, including most kids, won't go near them. I'm not above adding a bit of sweetness (and pork fat!) to greens to make them more appealing to more people.

This pretty green can be braised, too, but boiling it until just tender, lets you drain excess moisture (and it's quick). Tuscan kale usually comes in small bunches weighing 8 to 9 oz/225 to 255 g. If your bunches are slightly bigger (up to 10 oz/285 g), that's fine for this recipe. Any more, and you'd have to up the pancetta, ginger, and maple.

KOSHER SALT	1 TBSP UNSALTED BUTTER
1 BUNCH (*8 to 9 oz/ 225 or 255 g*) TUSCAN KALE (*a.k.a. cavalo nero or black kale*)	1½ TSP CHOPPED FRESH GINGER
1 OZ/30 G VERY THINLY SLICED PANCETTA (*3 or 4 slices*)	1 TSP PURE MAPLE SYRUP
	2 SMALL LEMON WEDGES

1   *Fill a wide 4- to 5-qt/3.8- to 4.7-L pot* two-thirds full of water. Add 2 tsp salt and bring to a boil. Remove the ribs from the kale. Grab the rib with one hand and rip the two leafy sides away from it with the other. Cut or rip the leaves into two or three smaller pieces. You'll have about 4 oz/115 g of greens. Add the greens to the boiling water and start timing immediately. Taste a leaf after 4 minutes. It shouldn't be tough or rubbery. If it is, cook for 1 to 2 minutes more. Drain the kale very thoroughly in a strainer in the sink. Press down on the kale to squeeze out some excess liquid.

2   *Put a medium (9- to 10-in/23- to 25-cm) nonstick skillet* over medium-low heat and arrange the pancetta slices in the pan. Cook the pancetta until crisp and lightly browned, 6 to 8 minutes, flipping once or twice. Transfer to a paper towel–lined plate. Add the butter to the pan, and as soon as it melts, add the ginger and stir to soften it slightly in the butter, about 30 seconds. Remove the pan from the heat and add the maple syrup. Stir well.

3   *Lift the kale* from the strainer, squeezing one more time to release excess moisture, and add to the pan with the maple-ginger butter. Put the pan back over medium-low heat and toss the greens until well coated and slightly warmed, 30 seconds to 1 minute. Remove the pan from the heat, taste, and season very lightly with salt. Crumble the pancetta over the greens. Toss briefly to mix and transfer to a serving platter. Alternatively, transfer the greens to individual plates and crumble the pancetta over the top. Serve with the lemon wedges.

Serves 2

Warm Parmesan Fava Beans with Shallots and Mint

Quick fava beans—that's an oxymoron, as my friend Debbie likes to say. It's true that shelling fava beans and then blanching them to remove their outer skin is time-consuming. And after all that, you wind up with a very small pile of beans, though you started with an impressive pile of gangly pods. These are probably reasons enough not to include fava beans in this book, except that I love them! (And, of course, if you do come across some, you'll want to know what to do with them.) They are about as fresh and green as it gets, and the nutty flavor is incomparable.

To make things easier, I've suggested a simple and tasty preparation for them (they only spend a minute or so in a sauté pan after blanching and peeling). I've also suggested a way to stretch this dish—serving it on toasted bread—if you want to share your fava beans with more than one person. The favas-on-crostini option makes a nice appetizer, too.

Occasionally, you'll find shelled favas in specialty groceries, and this saves a little time (although they're not as fresh). Otherwise, just relax and give in to the peaceful pleasure of shucking and peeling, or enlist the help of a young sous-chef to do this while you fix the rest of dinner. I probably don't have to tell you that you could sip a nice glass of Chianti while you're prepping.

2¼ TSP KOSHER SALT

2 LB/910 G FAVA BEANS IN THE POD

4 SLICES BAGUETTE (*about ½ in/1.25 cm thick and 3 in/7.5 cm long; optional*)

EXTRA-VIRGIN OLIVE OIL *for brushing the bread (optional)*

2 TBSP UNSALTED BUTTER

⅓ CUP/35 G THINLY SLICED SHALLOTS

½ TSP SHERRY VINEGAR

2 TBSP CHOPPED FRESH MINT

3 TBSP FINELY GRATED PARMIGIANO-REGGIANO

{ Continued }

1   *Fill a large saucepan* halfway with water and 2 tsp of the salt. Bring the water to a boil. Put a few cups of ice in a medium mixing bowl and fill the bowl with cold water. Set a hand-held mesh strainer near the stove. Shuck the favas (remove the beans from their long, bulky pods). Put all of the favas in the boiling water and start timing immediately.

2   *Cook the favas* for 2 minutes if all of the beans are small, or 3 minutes if some or all of the beans are older and bigger. Turn off the heat, use the mesh strainer to transfer the favas to the ice-water bath, and let sit for a minute or two. Drain the ice water. Remove the outer coating of each fava by pinching one end of the bean and popping or slipping the bean out of the skin. (The two halves of the bean will separate.)

3   *If serving on crostini,* brush the top of each baguette slice with about ¼ tsp olive oil and grill or broil until lightly golden.

4   *In a medium (9- to 10-in/23- to 25-cm) nonstick skillet,* melt the butter over medium heat. Add the shallots and cook, stirring, until the shallots are softened and lightly browned (don't brown too much, as they become bitter), about 2 minutes. Add the fava beans and the remaining ¼ tsp salt and cook, stirring, just until the fava beans are heated through, 1 to 2 minutes. Add the sherry vinegar and toss the beans. Remove the pan from the heat and stir in 1½ Tbsp of the mint and 2½ Tbsp of the Parmigiano.

5   *Transfer the favas* to a serving dish or dinner plates or pile them loosely over and around the grilled bread. Garnish with the remaining ½ Tbsp mint and ½ Tbsp Parmigiano. Serve warm.

Serves 2 or, with crostini, 4

New Potato Salad with Fresh Peas, Lime, and Yogurt

I first made this salad with potatoes that had literally been pulled from the ground (at Morning Glory Farm on Martha's Vineyard) that morning. I also had some fresh peas, and the two seemed made for each other. I made a dressing that's a riff on one my friend and potato guru Molly Stevens makes for a lemony potato salad. She lightens her mayonnaise with lightly whipped cream; mine has Greek yogurt (and lime zest) instead.

I loved this salad the first time I made it, and I still do. To save time, you can quick-chill the potatoes in the fridge for 20 minutes before you mix them with the dressing. If you're not in a rush, you can let them cool gradually at room temperature. Either way, if you get the potatoes going first, you can easily make the dressing in the time it takes for the potatoes to cook and cool.

This salad has a really lively flavor (thanks to lots of lime) that would pair well with a grilled, butterflied leg of lamb with a spice rub on it. But it's a perfect potluck dish!

One note: I have found that when doubling the recipe, I need slightly more dressing than a double amount, so add an extra tablespoon each of mayo and yogurt.

1 LB/455 G BABY YUKON GOLD POTATOES, *quartered or cut into sixths for similarly sized pieces*

2½ TSP KOSHER SALT, *and more if needed*

1 LB/455 G FRESH PEAS IN THE POD, *shelled (yielding 1 cup/140 g peas)*

⅓ CUP/65 G MAYONNAISE

¼ CUP/55 G THICK GREEK-STYLE YOGURT *(full fat or 2%)*

1 TSP LOOSELY PACKED FINELY GRATED LIME ZEST *(from about 1 lime)*

½ TSP FRESH LIME JUICE

¼ CUP/20 G SLICED SCALLIONS *(white and light green parts)*

3 TBSP THINLY SLICED FRESH MINT LEAVES

FRESHLY GROUND BLACK PEPPER

1   *Put the potatoes* and 2 tsp of the salt in a large saucepan and cover with plenty of water. Bring to a boil, reduce the heat to a simmer, and cook until almost tender, about 10 minutes. Add the peas and cook for 2 to 3 minutes more. Drain the potatoes and peas carefully in a colander and rinse them gently with cool water for a few minutes. Spread the potatoes and peas out on a small rimmed sheet pan and refrigerate for 20 minutes to cool.

2   *Meanwhile,* whisk the mayonnaise, yogurt, lime zest, and lime juice in a medium mixing bowl. Add the cooled potatoes and peas, the scallions, 2 Tbsp of the mint, the remaining ½ tsp salt, and several grinds of fresh pepper. Mix gently but thoroughly with a silicone spatula. Taste and add a little more salt, if desired. Garnish with the remaining 1 Tbsp of mint.

Serves 4

Green Bean, Snap Pea, and Pesto Salad with Cherry Tomatoes and Fresh Mozzarella

For impromptu entertaining on a summer evening, this is your salad, your side dish, your everything. So just throw some steaks on the grill and you're all set. Or even better, start a beer-can chicken roasting on the grill while you make this salad. It will take you a little bit of time to prep the vegetables, but prepared pesto (preferably a good one from the farmers' market or one made locally) is a time-saver here. Actually, if you're not in the mood to make your own pesto over the summer, you should do a taste comparison of several brands to find your "house" pesto. That may seem kind of crazy—buying several and tasting them side by side—but you will be blown away by the differences. Some of the national brands are, well, to be polite, not good. Some are overly salty, some have no basil flavor (if you get stuck with one of those, just add more fresh basil to this salad). But more often these days, you can find good locally made pesto in neighborhood and farmers' markets.

You may not be in the habit of using whole or torn herb leaves in a salad, but with basil, in particular, larger pieces give you a welcome burst of flavor without the bitterness that comes when basil is chopped too much (especially with a dull knife). I like the mozzarella balls that are about the size of a large cherry tomato, because when quartered, they make nice little bite-size wedges. But you can certainly use any fresh mozzarella and cut it into appropriately sized pieces. If you can't find yellow wax beans or snap peas, you can substitute green beans (fresh, slim ones, please) for either.

KOSHER SALT

8 OZ/225 G YELLOW WAX BEANS, *trimmed and halved lengthwise*

8 OZ/225 G SUGAR SNAP PEAS, *tails removed*

8 OZ/225 G SMALL RED AND YELLOW CHERRY TOMATOES OR GRAPE TOMATOES, *halved*

6 OZ/170 G MINI–MOZZARELLA BALLS *(1 in/2.5 cm), quartered*

¼ CUP/60 ML PREPARED BASIL PESTO

1 TSP WHITE BALSAMIC VINEGAR

½ TSP FRESH LEMON JUICE, *and more if needed*

1 TBSP EXTRA-VIRGIN OLIVE OIL

⅓ CUP/45 G TOASTED PINE NUTS *(see tip on page 36)*

20 TO 30 LARGE FRESH BASIL LEAVES, *torn into smaller pieces*

FRESHLY GROUND BLACK PEPPER

1 *Fill a large saucepan* two thirds full with water and add 2 tsp salt. Arrange a few layers of dish towels on a work surface or a sheet pan to drain the beans and peas. Add the beans to the boiling water and begin timing immediately. Boil until the beans are tender to the bite, 4 to 8 minutes. (Begin tasting after 4 minutes; the timing varies greatly, depending on the age of the beans and how quickly your burner returns the water to a boil.) Use tongs to lift the beans out of the water and spread them out on the towels to let them cool and to let excess moisture evaporate. Put the snap peas in the boiling water and cook until they're bright green and just slightly softened, about 2 minutes. Drain on towels and let cool.

2 *Season both the tomatoes* and the mozzarella with a pinch or two of salt. Put them in a large mixing bowl and add the wax beans, snap peas, and ¾ tsp salt. In a small bowl, whisk together the pesto, vinegar, ½ tsp lemon juice, and olive oil. Pour over the vegetables and mix and toss well. Add the pine nuts and basil and season with several grinds of fresh pepper. Toss well and let the vegetables sit for 5 to 10 minutes. Toss again and taste, adding more salt, pepper, or lemon juice as needed.

Serves 6

Chapter 8

No Cooking

METHOD: No cooking

EQUIPMENT: Mixing bowl or salad bowl, sharp knives, whisk

HEAT: None!

....

No Cooking: How It Works

Sometimes I can be a little slow on the uptake. When I first outlined this book, it didn't occur to me that one of the best techniques for "cooking" vegetables is no cooking at all. I know, you'd think that with all the excitement about raw food these days (and the fact that I practically live off tomato salads in the summer), I would have thought of this sooner. But I was so focused on how to help you all learn to cook delicious vegetables that I didn't really think of "no cooking" as a technique.

Fortunately, I usually figure this stuff out sooner or later. So I'm happy to present you with a chapter that will provide relief—from both the stove and from the heat of summer, when most of these recipes will jump into play.

While tomatoes are certainly my favorite "no cook" vegetable (though I also like them roasted!), there are plenty of other vegetables—such as carrots, cucumbers, cabbage, and spinach—that are delicious raw. Of course, if you were just going to eat these raw, you wouldn't need a recipe. Where uncooked vegetables really star is in salads and slaws with yummy vinaigrettes and dressings (see the recipe list on page 137). Many of my recipes were inspired by a desire to do better than the standard fare. For instance, I've never liked carrot salad, which I've found bland and mushy. My Double Lemon Ginger Carrot Salad is not only delicious, but it also takes advantage of my new favorite (cheap) tool, the hand-held julienne peeler, to make crisp, pretty strips of carrots. That's just one example of how taking a fresh and flavorful approach to dressing raw vegetables can make a big difference.

So while there's no big technique to master in this chapter, your success with these recipes will depend, in part, on choosing the freshest vegetables and herbs you can get your hands on. These recipes use a lot of herbs, so even if you're not a gardener, consider keeping a pot or two of basil and mint on your back step in the warmer months so that you don't have to constantly buy fresh herbs. And do get in the habit of patronizing your local farmers' market on a weekly basis. Aside from all the obvious reasons to support your market, you'll be pleased and amazed to find out how much longer those vegetables keep. They're just that much fresher to begin with.

In this chapter, you'll find tomato salad (surprise!), groovy slaws, and a few updates for classics like cucumber salad and spinach salad. You'll also get a little help remembering how good avocados are. I also think you'll really like the foundation recipe that starts off this chapter. It's a cross between a salad and a salsa, and can just as easily be a topping for grilled fish as it could be a side salad for steak or chicken.

Foundation Recipe for No-Cooking

This is a fun approach for a foundation recipe: Basically, it's a design-it-yourself salsa disguised as a salad. (It can go either way, depending on what size you cut everything.) You won't find a list of vegetables for the ingredient options, just choose vegetables and fruits that will all mingle and marry together well because they are fairly high in moisture content. So you will see nary a carrot or a broccoli floret in this recipe; it's all about tomatoes and cucumbers and summer fruit (and fresh herbs, of course). I think avocado is an important ingredient, because its texture and richness help balance the cooler vegetables and fruits. But you could certainly also make a nice version of one of these salads without the avocado.

I'd suggest that you cut everything into fairly small pieces once you've made your choices. (I like ½-inch/1.25-cm dice, but the "dice" don't have to be perfect.) And you could certainly cut larger pieces if you want to make a chunky salad, though I'd opt for the cucumbers over the squash in that case. (I think raw squash is best small.) Or you could cut everything smaller if you want to use this as, say, a topping for fish steaks for a party. The only thing you really need to do is to try to keep everything about the same size; the salad will not only look pretty but will also be easy to eat.

I also suggest that you take the seeds out of larger tomatoes. This isn't absolutely necessary, but it will make a neater salad when everything gets stirred together. Just cut the tomatoes in half and poke and prod the seeds out with your fingers.

Try to mix this salad as close to serving time as possible. Stir gently with a silicone spatula, and use as much of the dressing as you like; you may not need it all. After the salad is mixed, taste it not just for salt, but also for brightness and sweetness. You can always add a little squeeze of lime or a dash of orange juice if necessary. Be sure to use two or more herbs for the most interesting salad, and don't forget the bit of radish or jicama for crunch.

You've probably guessed by now that this salad is pretty darn versatile. You could make a tomato, cucumber, mango, and avocado salad to go with steak; a tomato, nectarine, and jicama salad to go with grilled shrimp; or a tomato, zucchini, peach, and avocado salad to go with grilled chicken. (Obviously I have grilling on the brain, but you could use one of these with roasted salmon or chicken, too.)

{ Continued }

Dressing

3 TBSP EXTRA-VIRGIN OLIVE OIL

1 TBSP FRESH ORANGE JUICE

2 TSP FRESH LIME JUICE

1 TSP HONEY

KOSHER SALT

Salad

2 OR 3 SMALL HEIRLOOM TOMATOES OR PLUM TOMATOES *(8 to 10 oz/225 to 285 g total), seeded and cut into small dice; or 8 oz/225 g small cherry tomatoes, quartered*

1 SMALL CUCUMBER *(7 to 8 oz/200 to 225 g), ends trimmed, peeled, cored, and cut into small dice; or 1 small zucchini or summer squash (7 to 8 oz/200 to 225 g), unpeeled, cut into small dice*

2 PEACHES OR NECTARINES, 3 PLUMS, OR 1 MANGO *(about 10 oz/285 g total), pitted and cut into small dice; OR CANTALOUPE OR HONEYDEW MELON (about 6 oz/170 g), cut into small dice*

1 AVOCADO *(about 10 oz/285 g), peeled, pitted, and cut into small dice*

2 SMALL RADISHES *(about 1 oz/30 g total), quartered and thinly sliced; OR JICAMA (about 2 oz/60 g), peeled, cut into small thin slices*

3 TBSP OF A COMBINATION OF AT LEAST 2 CHOPPED FRESH HERBS *(mint, basil, cilantro, or parsley)*

½ TSP KOSHER SALT

1   *To make the dressing:* in a small bowl, whisk together the olive oil, orange juice, lime juice, honey, and a good pinch of salt.

2   *To make the salad:* in a medium mixing bowl, combine your choice of tomatoes, cucumber or squash, fruit, the avocado, your choice of radish or jicama, and the herbs. Add the salt and drizzle most of the dressing over all. Toss well and taste. Add the remaining dressing and/or more salt, if needed. Taste again and adjust seasonings, if necessary. Transfer to a serving bowl.

Serves 4 to 6

"Go Green" Simple, Sassy Slaw

This slaw is just a beautiful thing—at its very simplest, it's just lime juice, salt, sugar, and savoy cabbage (the pretty, crinkly one). So incredibly easy, and just the thing to tuck into a fish taco (or even a chicken or beef taco). But since I like to complicate matters, I've added cilantro and scallions in this recipe to make the slaw more of a side dish. You can also add a bit of minced serrano pepper if you like, and a tablespoon of sour cream for a creamier feel. If you're feeling fancy, top it with toasted pepitas (Mexican pumpkin seeds).

Once the lime juice hits the cabbage, it will take a few minutes for the cabbage to soften and lose its raw texture. I find 15 to 20 minutes is about right (especially for a weeknight), but how "wilted" you want your slaw is really a matter of personal preference. The good news is that this slaw stays fresh tasting and somewhat crisp feeling even after it has sat for a bit. I've even eaten this the next day and loved it.

½ **SMALL HEAD SAVOY CABBAGE** *(about 8 oz/225 g), cored and thinly sliced*

3 TBSP FRESH LIME JUICE

2 TSP SUGAR

½ TSP KOSHER SALT

2 TBSP CHOPPED FRESH CILANTRO

2 TBSP FINELY CHOPPED SCALLIONS *(white and green parts)*

¼ TO ½ TSP MINCED SERRANO PEPPER *(optional)*

2 TO 3 TBSP TOASTED PEPITAS *(Mexican pumpkin seeds, optional; see tip on page 36)*

1 *In a medium mixing bowl,* combine the cabbage, lime juice, sugar, and salt. Let sit for 15 to 20 minutes, stirring occasionally. Add the cilantro, scallions, and serrano (if using). Stir well again, and let sit for 5 to 10 minutes more. Sprinkle with the toasted pepitas, if desired.

Serves 3 to 4

Heirloom Tomato, Summer Peach, and Fresh Herb Gazpacho Salad

If you're hitting the farmers' markets in late summer, sooner or later you're going to wind up with a bowl of peaches and a bowl of tomatoes next to each other on your kitchen counter. They're in season together, and they taste great together, with the sweetness of the peach balancing the acidity of the tomato—so go ahead and turn them into a salad. (But please don't make this salad in the off-season.) I call this easy summer dish a gazpacho salad not because it looks like one, but because you can roughly purée any leftovers in a blender, chill it, and you've got a delicious gazpacho.

The dressing for this salad has orange juice in it, but when I have it on hand, I like to substitute a store-bought mango smoothie drink (like Odwalla). When you toss the salad with the dressing, taste the juices, and if they aren't bright-tasting, add more balsamic vinegar or soy sauce. You can also add more mango drink if you need sweetness. If you can, try not to toss the salad until a few minutes before serving—while the flavor improves with sitting, the looks and texture do not. So if you're putting this out on a buffet, mix it very gently (right in its serving bowl) as close to serving time as possible. And remember to save some of the herbs for garnish. If you have edible flowers or purple basil leaves in your garden, this salad is the perfect destination for them.

2 LB/910 G HEIRLOOM TOMATOES (*a mix of sizes—including cherries—and colors is nice*)

1 LB/455 G RIPE PEACHES

½ SMALL RED ONION (*about 2 oz/60 g*)

2 TBSP EXTRA-VIRGIN OLIVE OIL

2 TBSP FRESH ORANGE JUICE OR MANGO SMOOTHIE DRINK, *and more if needed*

1 TBSP BALSAMIC VINEGAR, *and more if needed*

1 TSP SOY SAUCE, *and more if needed*

½ TSP FINELY GRATED LEMON ZEST

¼ TSP KOSHER SALT, *and more if needed*

½ CUP/15 G LIGHTLY PACKED SMALL WHOLE FRESH MINT AND BASIL LEAVES (*or large ones torn into smaller pieces*)

EDIBLE FLOWERS, *petals separated if large, for garnish (optional)*

{ Continued }

1   *Core the large tomatoes* and stem any cherry or tiny tomatoes. Cut the larger tomatoes into large, evenly sized pieces. To do this easily, first cut the tomatoes crosswise into thick slabs, and then cut the slabs into large dice (¾ to 1 in/2 to 2.5 cm wide). If the tomatoes are very irregularly shaped, just cut them into wedges and then cut the wedges in half. Cut the cherry or tiny tomatoes in half or into quarters. Put all of the tomatoes into a large, shallow serving bowl.

2   *Peel the peaches* with a paring knife and slice them off the pit into wedges (whatever size you like, depending on the size of your peach). Add the peaches to the bowl. Slice the onion lengthwise as thinly as you can and add it to the bowl, too.

3   *Whisk together the olive oil,* 2 Tbsp orange juice, 1 Tbsp balsamic vinegar, 2 tsp soy sauce, lemon zest, and ¼ tsp salt. Pour the dressing over the tomatoes and peaches. Add half of the herbs, season with salt, and toss gently but thoroughly. Taste the juices and add more vinegar, soy sauce, and orange juice if you need to. (You can let the salad sit for a few more minutes and taste and season again if you like.) Before serving, toss again and sprinkle with the remaining herbs and the flowers (if using).

Serves 6

Cucumber Salad with Greek Yogurt, Lime, and Honey

Super-fast and refreshing, this recipe is my version of a salad that shows up in Greek and Indian cuisines. I've taken cues from both, but mine relies on the wonderfully thick Greek-style yogurt that you can now get in many groceries. (I like Fage Total brand.) If you haven't tried this type of yogurt yet, I think you'll like it. It's luscious and delicious on its own with a little honey, and it also makes a good substitute for sour cream on baked potatoes.

With yogurt, cucumbers, and limes on hand, you can put this salad together in about 15 minutes. I don't recommend trying to make it ahead. The cucumbers and yogurt tend to weep as they sit. If this happens, carefully drain away the excess liquid. The toasted pine nuts are an optional garnish. The nutty flavor and textural contrast is nice, but the clean, bright flavors of the salad are lovely without them, too.

Serve this cooling salad with something spicy—on a weeknight, that might be spice-rubbed lamb kebabs, and on a weekend perhaps a curry or another spicy stew.

2 MEDIUM CUCUMBERS (*1¼ to 1½ lb/ 570 to 680 g total*)

⅓ CUP/20 G THINLY SLICED SCALLIONS (*white and light green parts; 3 or 4 medium*)

¾ CUP/165 G GREEK-STYLE YOGURT (*full fat*)

2 TBSP CHOPPED FRESH MINT, PLUS 1 OR 2 FRESH SPRIGS FOR GARNISH

¼ TSP PACKED FINELY GRATED LIME ZEST

1 TBSP PLUS 1 TSP FRESH LIME JUICE

2 TSP HONEY

¼ TSP GROUND CORIANDER

¼ TSP KOSHER SALT

2 TBSP COARSELY CHOPPED TOASTED PINE NUTS (*optional; see tip on page 36*)

1   *Trim the ends off* the cucumbers and peel them. First cut them in half crosswise into two shorter pieces for easier handling. Then cut each half in half lengthwise and scrape out the seeds with a spoon. Slice the cucumbers across into thin half-moons. Put the cucumbers and the scallions in a mixing bowl.

2   *In a smaller bowl,* whisk together the yogurt, chopped mint, lime zest, lime juice, honey, coriander, and salt. Spoon the mixture into the bowl of cucumbers and scallions and gently fold and mix with a silicone spatula until the ingredients are well combined. Transfer to a serving bowl and garnish with the mint sprigs and toasted pine nuts (if using).

Serves 4 to 6

Double-Lemon Ginger Carrot Salad

This salad is easy, very easy. When I was working on this chapter, for a while I thought that there just wasn't going to be a carrot salad. That seemed like a shame, since good, sweet carrots are delicious raw. The problem was that I hated the texture of grated carrots—too mushy. But once I got my hand-held julienne peeler, it was easy to make quick little carrot strips. The tool can be a bit awkward on thin carrots, so I'd stick to medium-thick or larger for this recipe. (You can, of course, use a mandoline, but the peeler is much more finger-friendly.) Munch on the small pieces that are left after peeling.

I love lemon and ginger with carrots, but I wanted something just a little different here, so I used minced crystallized ginger in the dressing. Delicious! The little bit of sugar melts into the lemon and orange juices and mellows the tart lemon zest and the sharp ginger. It's perfect with the carrots. Be sure to start with good, sweet (preferably organic or locally grown) carrots, as old carrots turn bitter and will affect the taste of the salad.

I wanted this recipe to be super-quick, so it only makes 3 servings; but you can easily double it. Try serving the carrots scooped into Bibb lettuce leaves, or rolled in rice paper.

8 TO 9 OZ/225 TO 255 G MEDIUM OR LARGE CARROTS, *preferably organic, peeled*

1 TBSP PEANUT OIL

2 TSP MINCED OR FINELY CHOPPED CRYSTALLIZED GINGER

2 TSP FRESH ORANGE JUICE

2 TSP FRESH LEMON JUICE

½ TSP FINELY GRATED LEMON ZEST

½ TSP MINCED OR FINELY CHOPPED SHALLOT

¼ TSP KOSHER SALT

2 TBSP COARSELY CHOPPED FRESH PARSLEY (*or cilantro, if you prefer*)

1. *Trim the ends* of the carrots and lay them on a cutting board. Peel each one into thin julienne strips with a hand-held julienne peeler. It's easiest to prop the carrot against the cutting board while peeling and to alternate peeling halfway from one end and then halfway from the other end. Continue peeling until you cannot peel any more. The strips will be inconsistently sized for this salad, and that's okay. You can even use the thinnest, most shredded pieces. Put all of the carrots in a medium bowl.

2. *In a small bowl,* whisk together the peanut oil, crystallized ginger, orange juice, lemon juice, lemon zest, and shallot. Let sit for a few minutes so the shallots soften and the ginger disperses, and whisk again. Sprinkle the salt over the carrots and drizzle and scrape the dressing over them. Toss and mix well, and let sit for about 5 minutes (10 to 15 minutes at the most), tossing occasionally. Mix in the parsley and serve the carrot salad with a slotted spoon.

Serves 3

Simple Avocado and Herb Salad for One or More

Sometimes I get a craving for avocado, so I slice one up and season it with salt, pepper, a squirt of lemon juice, and a little extra-virgin olive oil. I stand at the kitchen counter and savor every bite. It's then that I'm reminded that an avocado isn't just a salad or dip ingredient—it's wonderful in its own right. And it's the perfect thing for a simple but delicious side dish for a summer dinner. So I offer this basic recipe—with a few flavor choices—for dressing and serving an avocado as a reminder not to forget about these amazingly nutritious, colorful, and satisfying fruits. (Yes, technically, it's a fruit.) You can vary the flavors of the dressing as you like by choosing either lime or lemon juice, mint or cilantro, scallions or ginger.

For a side dish, I think half of an avocado is a good-size portion, so the amounts I've suggested below are enough to dress one half. Obviously you can double or triple this recipe, or whatever you like, to serve bigger portions or more people. I like to slice the avocado and fan the slices, but if your avocado is a bit overripe, cutting it into large dice will be easier. Either way, if you arrange the avocado with a bit of Bibb lettuce or mâche, you can disguise messy cutting and make the presentation a little fancier at the same time.

Avocado's a natural with shrimp (seared, grilled, or even poached), but I bet you'd love one of these with a grilled chicken breast and some sliced ripe beefsteak tomatoes on a summer night.

1½ TSP EXTRA-VIRGIN OLIVE OIL

½ TSP FRESH LEMON OR LIME JUICE

½ TSP COARSELY CHOPPED FRESH PARSLEY, MINT, OR CILANTRO

½ TSP MINCED SCALLION (*white and light green parts; optional*)

¼ TSP GRATED FRESH GINGER (*optional*)

½ TSP FRESH ORANGE JUICE (*optional*)

½ AVOCADO, *halved lengthwise and pitted, but not peeled (see tip)*

KOSHER SALT

FRESHLY GROUND BLACK PEPPER

1 SMALL INNER LEAF BIBB LETTUCE, *or a few leaves of mâche*

{ Continued }

1   *Whisk together the olive oil,* lemon juice, and herbs. If desired, add either the scallions or the ginger and whisk again. (Add the orange juice, if desired, just before serving.)

2   *To serve the avocado sliced:* Use a sharp chef's knife to slice through the avocado half crosswise at ¼-in/6.5-mm intervals, cutting through the skin almost completely. Turn the avocado half over on the cutting board and peel away the skin. Slide a knife under the avocado and transfer it to a very small plate (or the side of a dinner plate). Fan the slices out as neatly as possible. Season the avocado with a generous pinch or two of salt and a little bit of pepper. Arrange a few leaves of Bibb lettuce over or to one side of the avocado. Drizzle all of the dressing over the avocado and lettuce and serve.

     To serve the avocado diced: Use a sharp chef's knife to slice through the avocado half crosswise at ¾-in/2-cm intervals and then lengthwise in thirds to create large dice. Remove the dice from the skin and transfer them to a small bowl. Add the dressing and toss well. Put the Bibb lettuce in small bowls and arrange the diced avocado in it and serve.

Serves 1

Tip: For easier cutting—and peeling—trim a sliver off each end of the avocado before cutting it in half lengthwise all the way around.

Colorful Chinese Kick-Slaw

I call this kick-slaw because it's got kicky flavors—ginger, garlic, lime, and sesame. I used to make a version of this when I cooked in the kitchen of a gourmet market in Newport, Rhode Island, years ago. We sold lots and lots of it in the summertime to folks on their way to the beach. It's not only refreshing but colorful, too, with the red cabbage, orange carrots, and green snow peas. I've included this recipe, along with another slaw in this chapter, because I've never been a fan of ordinary mayo slaws.

Don't be daunted by the long ingredient list—yes, there's a little slicing and chopping to do, but then you're done. (As you can see by the length of the directions, this ain't hard.) The flavors hold up well, so it could be made ahead. But I think the texture suffers some, so I recommend assembling it pretty close to serving time. Put this out for any summer buffet, or use it as a bed for grilled flank steak or swordfish.

½ **SMALL HEAD RED CABBAGE** (*about 9 oz/255 g*), *cored and thinly sliced*

5 OZ/140 G **SNOW PEAS,** *tails trimmed, each cut sharply on a diagonal into 3 pieces*

4 OZ/115 G **CARROTS,** *shredded (use the large holes of a box grater)*

½ **TSP KOSHER SALT**

2 **TSP MINCED GARLIC**

1 **TBSP FINELY CHOPPED FRESH GINGER**

1 **TBSP FRESH LIME JUICE**

2 **TBSP ORANGE JUICE**

2½ **TBSP HOISIN SAUCE**

1 **TBSP SOY SAUCE**

½ **TSP SESAME OIL**

1½ **TBSP PEANUT OIL**

¼ **CUP/15 G CHOPPED FRESH CILANTRO**

1   *In a large mixing bowl,* combine the cabbage, snow peas, and carrots. Sprinkle with the salt and mix well.

2   *In a small bowl,* combine the garlic, ginger, lime juice, orange juice, hoisin sauce, soy sauce, sesame oil, and peanut oil. Mix well and pour over the cabbage mixture. Mix thoroughly, add the cilantro, and mix again. Serve at room temperature.

Serves 4 or 5

Big-Bowl Spinach and Snow Pea Salad with Cashews

This big, green, fresh salad is a cross between a salad and a slaw. Baby spinach leaves and shredded Napa cabbage play the leafy roles here, and sliced snow peas and slivered Granny Smith apples do the crispy-juicy thing. Roasted cashews add crunch, and the sesame dressing has a surprise ingredient—apple cider—that makes this sweet and tangy at the same time. Altogether, this feels like a close cousin to the popular Chinese chicken salad (but without the chicken!).

This recipe yields a lot, so make it when a crowd is coming. You can make the dressing up to a day ahead, and you can prep the rest of the ingredients an hour ahead. I think you'll want to toss close to serving time, in order to keep the salad fresh looking. However, like many slaw-type salads, this actually is tastier after it sits for a bit. So if you don't mind the spinach wilting, make it 10 to 20 minutes ahead and toss it every so often. Either way, this will be delicious on the first helping—or the second. Serve it with a big platter of sliced, grilled pork loin coated with a Chinese five-spice rub.

2 TBSP PEANUT OIL	6 OZ/170 G BABY SPINACH LEAVES
2 TBSP APPLE CIDER	10 OZ/285 G THINLY SLICED NAPA CABBAGE
2 TSP LOW-SODIUM SOY SAUCE	
2 TSP FRESH LIME JUICE	4 OZ/115 G SNOW PEAS, *tails trimmed, each cut on a sharp diagonal into 3 pieces*
2 TSP HOISIN SAUCE	
1 TSP SESAME OIL	1 GRANNY SMITH APPLE, *unpeeled but cored, and cut into matchsticks*
1 TSP BALSAMIC VINEGAR	⅔ CUP/100 G COARSELY CHOPPED SALTED, ROASTED CASHEWS (*see page 36*)
½ TSP GRATED FRESH GINGER	
½ TSP DIJON MUSTARD	¼ TSP KOSHER SALT, *and more if needed*

1 *In a small bowl,* combine the peanut oil, apple cider, soy sauce, lime juice, hoisin sauce, sesame oil, balsamic vinegar, ginger, and mustard. Whisk well.

2 *Put the spinach leaves* in a very large mixing bowl. Put the cabbage on top of the spinach. Add the snow peas, apple, and cashews. (If making ahead, you can cover with damp paper towels, wrap in plastic, and refrigerate for up to an hour.)

3 *Sprinkle the ¼ tsp salt* over the salad ingredients, pour on all of the dressing, and mix and toss well (with your hands or tongs) to combine thoroughly. Let sit for a few minutes, toss again and taste. Add more salt, if necessary. Toss again and serve.

Serves 8

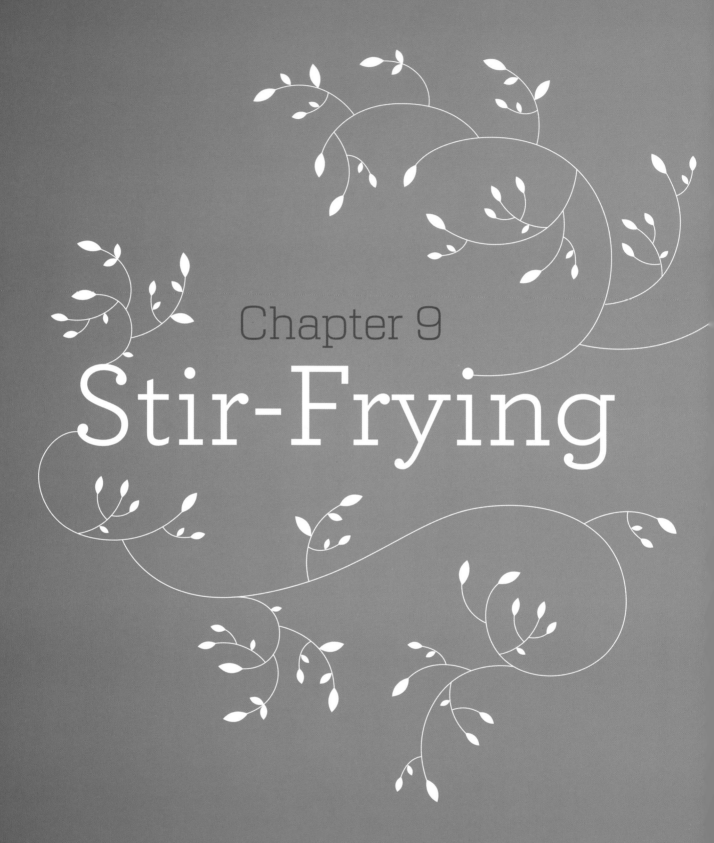

Chapter 9
Stir-Frying

METHOD: Stir-frying

EQUIPMENT: 12-in/30.5-cm nonstick stir-fry pan, tongs, silicone spatula

HEAT: The stove top, cranked up

Stir-Frying: How It Works

In my next life, I'm going to be a vegetable cheerleader and stand on the kitchen sidelines, jumping up and down chanting "Stir-Fry! Stir-Fry! Stir-Fry!" I feel like I have to make up for the poor karma I initially brought to this handy cooking technique. It's just that I had a hard time understanding that stir-frying (at home, in a stir-fry pan) is not wok-searing (at a restaurant, in a flame-enveloped wok).

I really had no excuse, because I had learned the truth years ago. None other than Barbara Tropp, the late Chinese cooking expert, wrote an article in *Fine Cooking* magazine explaining that most home cooks are better off with a flat-bottomed stir-fry pan. Woks, she explained, are designed to be surrounded by flames—not raised above them on a hot burner. On a home stove, there's no way for heat to climb up the sides of the wok, so the only stuff that cooks is what's in the very bottom. (Of course if you had a built-in wok burner, you wouldn't have this problem.) Tropp even admitted that she really liked stir-fry pans because of their generous size and shape. (They are wider and more bowl-shaped than a flat-bottom wok.)

The shape—that wide bowl—is what finally won me over. So much room to toss and flip and stir! And so much pan surface that you never have to worry that some lonesome vegetable won't get in contact with the heat. In fact, once I realized that a stir-fry pan both browns and steams at the same time, I almost felt like I was cheating every time I cooked with it. How easy is this?, I thought. Heat up some oil, put the stuff in, stir it 'round and 'round. Add extra flavors, stir some more, eat.

Of course there's a little bit more to it than that (see below), but the important thing is that the results are deeply delicious vegetables. They don't have quite the crisp-tender texture of their wok cousins, but they don't require a bonfire either.

Here are some stir-frying tricks I've learned:

- Buy a mid-priced nonstick stir-fry pan of average weight. Mine is a Circulon, and I love it. You don't want an expensive stir-fry pan; they're too heavy to lift, often have a smaller capacity than less-expensive pans, and sometimes aren't nonstick (which these recipes were developed for). You also don't want a cheapo, as they have inferior nonstick surfaces that deteriorate quickly and can conduct heat unevenly.

- Cut vegetables in a way that maximizes surface area for browning. For instance, I always cut broccoli and cauliflower florets in half to create flat sides that can have more contact with the pan.

- Use medium or medium-high heat to preheat the oil in your pan. An empty stir fry pan shouldn't be heated on high because it can adversely affect the nonstick surface. But once the vegetables go in (and the pan is quite crowded in most of these recipes), the pan temperature will drop, so you'll then want to turn up the heat to high for a chance at the best browning.

- Use peanut oil, canola oil, or grapeseed oil for stir-frying. Butter, olive oil, and other fats have smoke points that are too low for the high-heat of stir-frying.

- The stir-fry pan is great for Chinese-style vegetable dishes (like the Stir-Fried Broccoli, Mushrooms, and Onions with Tasty Sauce on page 166), but don't underestimate its usefulness for other kinds of side dishes. I cook Swiss chard in it, because I can stir-fry the stems first and wilt the leaves at the end.

- When you're making a sauce in the pan, keep in mind that the sauce will become too thick or scorch very quickly if kept over a hot burner for long. Depending on how full the pan is (and therefore how hot it is), you may need to remove the pan from the heat just before or after adding the sauce ingredients. But since a cornstarch-thickened sauce will need some heat to activate the thickening, you might need to keep the pan over the burner for a few seconds. This is something you'll have to gauge on your own stove with your own pan. Regardless of the recipe, put a serving dish or platter next to the stove. That way, when the dish is finished, you can quickly transfer it out of the pan to prevent overcooking.

Well, I think I'll stop here. If I go on, I'll risk making you suspicious that this is more complicated than I said it is. And it isn't. So just get out your pan and start stir-frying. For fun, try the foundation recipe, as it gives you lots of options to customize your own dish. Or just dive into one of the other recipes. My favorite? The Stir-Fried Baby Bok Choy with Golden Garlic and Silky Sauce (page 161).

VEGETABLES FOR STIR-FRYING

HEARTY VEGETABLE	WAY TO CUT
Broccoli florets	1 to 1½ in/2.5 to 3.75 cm long, ¾ to 1 in/2 to 2.5 cm wide, with one flat cut side
Brussels sprouts	cut in half lengthwise and then into thirds to make six pieces
Carrots	cut on the diagonal into pieces about 1½ in/3.75 cm long and ¼ in/6.5 mm thick
Cauliflower florets	1 in/2.5 cm long, about ¾ in/2 cm wide, with one flat cut side
Green beans	cut on a diagonal into 2 or 3 pieces

AROMATIC VEGETABLE	WAY TO CUT
Bell peppers	cut into 1-in/2.5-cm squares or long slices about ½ in/1.25 cm thick
Brown mushrooms such as cremini (baby bella)	quartered
Red onions	cut into 1-in/2.5-cm squares or long slices about ½ in/1.25 cm thick

Foundation Recipe for Stir-Frying

You'll have a lot of fun with this recipe, customizing your own mix as you please. The ingredients list may look long, but the sauce comes together in a jiffy. In this foundation recipe, I've limited the main vegetable choices somewhat so they will all cook together in the same amount of time. But you can use more than one in the same dish, as long as your total is still about 10 oz/285 g. And I've added a second vegetable—a lesser amount of mushrooms, bell peppers, or red onions—because I think these aromatic vegetables not only boost the interest in a stir-fry but also provide moisture to help the other vegetables cook. As I mention in the introduction to this chapter, cooking at home in a stir-fry pan involves both direct and indirect heat, so there is a bit of steaming that goes on simultaneously with searing. You only need to stir occasionally, though.

The sauce I've included here will make good use of the pantry items that I've suggested you keep on hand (see page 14). It will give your stir-fry a nice Chinese-restaurant flavor, but it's not absolutely necessary. A drier stir-fry can be tasty, so if you want to skip the sauce, consider just adding 1 tsp butter and 1 or 2 Tbsp chopped fresh herbs like cilantro, basil, Thai basil, mint, or parsley at the end. (Don't ever skip the ginger and garlic, though, and as far as I'm concerned, the more ginger the better.) Without the sauce, you'll probably have to add a bit more salt, too.

1 TBSP LOW-SODIUM CHICKEN BROTH

1 TBSP HOISIN SAUCE

1 TBSP OYSTER SAUCE

2 TSP FRESH ORANGE JUICE

1 TSP LOW-SODIUM SOY SAUCE

1 TSP RICE WINE OR SHERRY

½ TSP ASIAN SESAME OIL

½ TSP CORNSTARCH

2 TBSP PEANUT OIL

10 OZ/285 G YOUR CHOICE OF HEARTY VEGETABLE *(trimmed; see the table on page 156 for choices and how to cut them)*

4 OZ/115 G YOUR CHOICE OF AROMATIC VEGETABLE *(trimmed; see the table on page 156 for choices and how to cut them)*

½ TSP KOSHER SALT

2 OZ/60 G BABY SPINACH LEAVES OR BEAN SPROUTS *(optional)*

1 TSP MINCED FRESH GINGER

1 TSP MINCED FRESH GARLIC

2 TBSP THINLY SLICED SCALLIONS *(white and light green parts; optional)*

⅛ TSP CRUSHED RED PEPPER FLAKES *(optional)*

1 *In a small bowl,* combine the broth, hoisin sauce, oyster sauce, orange juice, soy sauce, rice wine, sesame oil, and cornstarch. Whisk well to combine.

2 *In a large (12-in/30.5-cm) nonstick stir-fry pan,* heat the peanut oil over medium-high heat. When the oil is hot (it will loosen up), add all of the vegetables and the salt and turn the heat up to high. Toss the vegetables well with tongs to coat them with the oil. Cook, stirring occasionally, until the vegetables are softened, shrunken, and browned in spots, 8 to 12 minutes, depending on the vegetables. Add the spinach leaves (if using) and stir until thoroughly combined and lightly wilted, about 30 seconds. Add the ginger, garlic, scallions (if using), and red pepper flakes (if using). Cook, stirring constantly, until the aromatics are well mixed and quite fragrant, about 1 minute. Whisk the sauce ingredients again and, with a silicone spatula, clear a space in the middle of the pan. Pour in the sauce and stir quickly and thoroughly to incorporate it and to let it thicken slightly, about 15 seconds. Remove the pan from the heat and immediately transfer the contents of the pan to a serving dish to prevent further cooking and to keep the sauce from scorching.

Serves 3 to 4

Stir-Fried Carrots with Ginger, Lime, and Cilantro

I think carrots and cilantro were made for each other. Add ginger, garlic, and lime, and you have a completely yummy carrot dish. The browning that happens in the stir-fry pan makes it that much better. This is another recipe that I could just sit down and eat all by myself for dinner, but if I were sharing, I'd serve these carrots with shrimp or grilled fish.

In this stir-fry, like many of the others in this chapter, the pan may look a little crowded when you start out. Not to worry; the carrots need a little crowding to release some steam, which will help them get tender. The big surface area of the stir-fry pan means there's plenty of room for browning. I find it's best not to stir too frequently, so that the vegetables have prolonged contact with the pan. In the end, some will be browner than others, and that's okay.

You can cut the carrots two ways, either as angle-cut coins or as sticks. The coins are much easier to cut than the sticks, but I prefer the texture and look of the sticks, and I think they cook slightly more evenly. Either way is fine. Both cilantro and lime vary in pungency, so I've given a range and you can add as much as you like.

1 LB/455 G SLIM CARROTS	1 TSP MINCED FRESH GARLIC
1 TBSP PEANUT OIL	½ TBSP UNSALTED BUTTER
½ YELLOW ONION (about 4 oz/115 g), halved crosswise and cut into thin strips	1½ TSP FRESH LIME JUICE
1 TSP KOSHER SALT	1 TO 2 TBSP CHOPPED FRESH CILANTRO, plus sprigs for garnish (optional)
2 TSP MINCED FRESH GINGER	½ LIME, cut into 4 pieces

1   *Trim and peel the carrots,* and then slice them thinly or cut them into sticks. If slicing, cut them on an angle into ovals between ⅛ and ¼ in/3.25 and 6.5 mm thick. Sticks should be between ¼ and ⅜ in/6.5 and 9.5 mm thick and 2 to 3 in/5 to 7.5 cm long.

2   *In a large (12-in/30.5-cm) nonstick stir-fry pan,* heat the peanut oil over medium-high heat. When the oil is hot (it will loosen up), add the carrots, onion, and salt and stir well with tongs. Turn the heat up to high and cook, stirring only occasionally and spreading out the vegetables after every stir, until the onion is limp and brown and the carrots are browned in places (they should have lost their stiffness, and some will be slightly blackened), 12 to 13 minutes.

3   *Turn the heat down to low,* add the ginger and garlic, and stir until fragrant, about 30 seconds. Turn off the heat, add the butter, and toss and stir gently until it melts. Stir in the lime juice and as much of the cilantro as you like. Serve each portion with a piece of lime, and garnish with cilantro sprigs, if desired.

Serves 4

Speedy Stir-Fried Asparagus with Toasted Garlic

This quick stir-fry for two delivers big flavor with very little effort. Cooked over high heat in an uncrowded pan, asparagus browns quickly and takes on an alluring nutty flavor. Letting the garlic brown only deepens the flavor, and makes this dry stir-fry plenty tasty without a sauce.

Keep an eye on the garlic when you're cooking it. You want to take it beyond the softening stage, but you don't want to burn it. When you begin to see browned garlic on the bottom of the pan, you can stir for just a few more seconds and you'll be done.

When I stir-fry asparagus, I always slice it thinly on a sharp diagonal. It not only looks pretty, but it also cooks more evenly and allows the cut surfaces of the stalks to brown. That distinctive flavor of browned asparagus—nutty, earthy, herby—always makes me want to pair it with something soft and creamy and custardy—polenta, an omelet, or a even a pillowy pasta like gnocchi or fresh tortellini, tossed in a bit of lemon butter.

2½ TSP PEANUT OIL	¼ TSP KOSHER SALT
8 OZ/225 G ASPARAGUS, *trimmed and thinly sliced on a sharp diagonal into pieces about 2 in/5 cm long*	1½ TSP MINCED FRESH GARLIC

1 *In a large (12-in/30.5-cm) nonstick stir-fry pan,* heat 2 tsp of the peanut oil over medium-high heat. When the oil is hot (it will loosen up and shimmer), add the asparagus and salt and turn the heat up to high. Stir the asparagus so that it's well coated with the oil and spread it out in the pan. Cook, without stirring at all for the first minute and only occasionally after that, until most of the asparagus are browned around the edges and somewhat shrunken (a few will be browned on the bottoms), 3 to 4 minutes. Add the remaining ½ tsp peanut oil and the garlic and cook, stirring constantly, until the garlic begins to turn brown, about 1 minute (You will see some browned garlic on the bottom of the pan, but not all of the garlic will be brown.) Immediately transfer the asparagus to a serving dish.

Serves 2

Stir-Fried Baby Bok Choy with Golden Garlic and Silky Sauce

Lovely little heads of baby bok choy make beautiful and tasty stir-fries. I like this vegetable so much that I've included two recipes for it in this book (see Cider-Braised Baby Bok Choy and Golden Apples on page 63), even though it isn't always as available as I wish it was. One tricky thing about buying baby bok choy, though, is that the little heads vary a lot in size. It's worth your time to pick through them at the store with two goals in mind: Choose heads that are close in size to each other, and choose the smallest heads. Then, weigh them to be sure you've got close to 12 oz/340 g.

Prepping the bok choy will take you a few minutes, but after that, the recipe comes together very quickly and easily. The garlic chips brown as the bok choy cooks, and with the mellow complement of oyster sauce, this recipe is a winner. For a party, I'd serve these with grilled salmon. But this is another recipe with such deep flavor that it would make a veggie-lover like me happy with just some basmati rice alongside.

---

12 OZ/340 G BABY BOK CHOY (*3 to 4 heads, each 6 to 7 in/15.25 to 17.75 cm long and 2 in/5 cm wide*)

1 TBSP OYSTER SAUCE

1 TBSP LOW-SODIUM CHICKEN BROTH

½ TSP CORNSTARCH

2 TBSP PEANUT OIL

2 LARGE OR EXTRA-LARGE GARLIC CLOVES, *sliced very thinly crosswise*

½ TSP KOSHER SALT

---

1 *Cut the bok choy lengthwise* into quarters if small (3 oz/85 g), and into six pieces if larger (4 oz/170 g). Wash them well by swishing them in a bowl of tepid water, and spin them dry. Put aside a serving dish on your counter.

2 *In a small bowl,* combine the oyster sauce, broth, and cornstarch.

3 *In a large (12-in/30.5-cm) nonstick stir-fry pan,* heat the peanut oil over medium heat. When the oil is hot (it will loosen up), add the garlic slices and break them up. Cook, stirring, just until fragrant, about 30 seconds. Add the bok choy to the pan. Season with the salt and turn the heat up to high. Using tongs, toss the bok choy with the oil to coat and to distribute the garlic slices.

4 *Cook, rotating and turning the bok choy* with tongs and spreading it out so that all of the stems have some contact with the pan as they cook, and so that the garlic doesn't all gather on the bottom of the pan, until all of the bok choy stems are browned in parts (the leaves will be wilted and browned), 9 to 12 minutes. Remove the pan from the heat and, using a silicone spatula, immediately stir the sauce as you pour it into the pan. As soon as the sauce thickens and begins to coat the vegetables, transfer the bok choy and the sauce to the serving dish.

Serves 3

Happy Stir-Fry of Zucchini, Corn, and Peanuts

This stir-fry is a fun and colorful combination of textures and flavors. It's a special dish, one you'd make for someone you're sweet on (as long as he or she isn't allergic to peanuts!). You could make this with pine nuts, too. I say special because the flavor payoff is big, but the prep takes a little time. The cooking goes fast, of course, so grab a helper for the prep. You won't need much else for dinner—a little grilled something, like a chicken breast or, even better, a few sea scallops—because this dish steals the show.

In this stir-fry, the peanuts go into (and come out of) the pan first. Keep a very close eye on them and stir constantly, as they brown quickly. When the vegetables go into the pan, the pan will look overcrowded. But as long as you've got your heat cranked up, they will still brown as they cook through. While you're stirring, occasionally spread the vegetables out against the pan for maximum contact. The corn will sometimes sputter, but stirring helps to minimize this.

1 LARGE ZUCCHINI *(10 to 11 oz/285 to 310 g)*

1¾ CUPS/245 G FRESH CORN KERNELS (FROM ABOUT 3 LARGE EARS; SEE TIP, PAGE 67)

6 LARGE SCALLIONS *(white and green parts), sliced ½ in/1.25 cm thick*

2 TSP THICK HOISIN SAUCE *(I like Lee Kum Kee brand)*

1 TSP FISH SAUCE

1 TSP FRESH LIME JUICE

1 TBSP FINELY CHOPPED FRESH GINGER

1½ TSP MINCED FRESH GARLIC

¼ TSP CHILI-GARLIC SAUCE

2 TBSP PEANUT OIL

⅓ CUP/50 G UNSALTED PEANUTS

1 TSP KOSHER SALT

1½ TBSP FINELY CHOPPED FRESH MINT

1½ TBSP CHOPPED FRESH CILANTRO

1   *Trim the ends off the zucchini* and cut it in half crosswise. Put one half on the cutting board, cut side down, and cut panels off all four sides, revealing the inner core of seeds. Discard the core, and cut the panels into medium (½-in/1.25-cm) dice. Repeat with the other half. Combine the zucchini, corn, and scallions in a bowl and set by the stove.

2   *In a small bowl,* combine the hoisin sauce, fish sauce, lime juice, and 1 tsp of water. Whisk to combine, and set by the stove. Combine the ginger, garlic, and chili-garlic sauce in another small bowl and set by the stove.

3   *Heat 1 Tbsp of the peanut oil* in a large (12-in/30.5-cm) stir-fry pan over medium heat. When the oil is hot (it will loosen up), add the peanuts and stir-fry until they all have browned in spots, 2 to 3 minutes. Watch carefully, as they go from browning to burning quickly. Remove the pan from the heat to stop the cooking and use a slotted spoon to transfer the peanuts (and any partial peanuts) to a plate or bowl.

4   *Add the remaining* 1 Tbsp of peanut oil to the pan and set the pan over medium-high heat. When the oil is hot (it will loosen up and shimmer), add the zucchini, corn, scallions, and salt. Turn the heat up to high and cook, stirring infrequently at first but more frequently as the vegetables start to brown, until the corn is all nicely browned and the zucchini is somewhat browned and starting to look translucent, 5 to 6 minutes.

5   *Add the ginger-garlic mixture* and stir-fry until well mixed, about 30 seconds. Add the hoisin mixture, scraping all of it out of its bowl, and immediately remove the pan from the heat. Stir to incorporate the sauce. Stir in the reserved peanuts, the mint, and cilantro. Mix well and transfer the vegetables to a serving platter to stop the cooking. Serve hot or warm.

Serves 3 to 4

Stir-Fried Bok Choy and Napa Cabbage with Black Bean Sauce

There are lots of delicious Chinese greens, but bok choy and Napa cabbage are two that are readily available in grocery stores, and they make fast, delicious stir-fries. The only frustrating thing is that two heads of this stuff (one of each) can feed an army. Sometimes you can buy half-heads, but if you do wind up bringing a lot home from the market, they will store well. In fact, to save on prep time later on, you can slice, wash, and dry the greens ahead. They'll keep in zip-top bags for several days. Doing this ahead makes this recipe super-fast, as the cooking time is less than 5 minutes.

If you do want to cook greens a few nights in a row, you can vary the recipe by replacing the onion with scallions, by adding ½ tsp chili-garlic sauce for a kick, or by adding chopped peanuts or toasted sesame seeds. However, don't be tempted to replace the black bean sauce with something like oyster sauce or hoisin. The greens naturally give off water as they cook (stir "frying" is a bit of a misnomer here) and the sauce gets a bit diluted. The pungent flavor of black bean sauce can stand up to it, and the delicious liquid then begs for rice. These greens would be good with oven-roasted boneless pork ribs.

2 TBSP BLACK BEAN SAUCE *(I like Lee Kum Kee brand)*

2 TSP FRESH ORANGE JUICE

1 TSP LOW-SODIUM SOY SAUCE

¾ TSP CORNSTARCH

½ TSP SESAME OIL

2 TSP PEANUT OIL

½ MEDIUM ONION *(3 to 4 oz/85 to 115 g), thinly sliced*

4 CUPS LIGHTLY PACKED SLICED NAPA CABBAGE *(about 6 oz/170 g; see tip)*

4 CUPS LIGHTLY PACKED SLICED BOK CHOY *(7 to 8 oz/200 to 225 g; see tip)*

¼ TSP KOSHER SALT

1 CUP *(about 2 oz/60 g)* **BEAN SPROUTS**

1 TSP MINCED FRESH GARLIC

2 TSP MINCED FRESH GINGER

1 *In a small bowl,* combine the black bean sauce, orange juice, soy sauce, cornstarch, and sesame oil. Whisk well to blend.

2 *In a large (12-in/30.5-cm) nonstick stir-fry pan,* heat 1 tsp of the peanut oil over medium-high heat. When the oil is hot (it will loosen up and shimmer), turn the heat up to high, add the onion, and cook, stirring frequently, until it's lightly browned, about 3 minutes.

3 *Add the remaining 1 tsp peanut oil,* the Napa cabbage, bok choy, and salt. Cook, stirring constantly, until the greens have mostly wilted, about 1 minute. Add the bean sprouts, garlic, and ginger and cook, stirring, until the aromatics are well distributed and fragrant and the greens are fully wilted, 30 to 45 seconds. With a silicone spatula, pour and scrape all of the sauce into the center of the pan and stir immediately. Remove the pan from the heat and continue to stir until the sauce is well distributed, 30 seconds to 1 minute. Transfer the greens to a serving platter and serve right away.

Serves 4

Tip: **To prep both greens, cut about 1 in/2.5 cm off the stem end and cut the head in half lengthwise. Cut out the core of the Napa cabbage. One at a time, put each Napa cabbage and bok choy half, cut side down, on a cutting board. Slice across (both the crunchy stem and the leafy green—don't worry about separating them) into ribbons about ½ in/1.25 cm thick.**

Stir-Fried Broccoli, Mushrooms, and Onions with Tasty Sauce

Broccoli is one of my favorite vegetables to stir-fry, because it develops such a complex, nutty flavor when it browns. This recipe has a particularly deep, rich flavor, not only because it includes mushrooms, but also because it features a sauce that combines oyster sauce, hoisin sauce, and soy sauce.

When I cut broccoli florets for a stir-fry, I first cut the florets away from the stem where they naturally separate from it. Then I take those florets and slice most of them in half (or even thirds). This does two things: It gives the floret one flat cut side, which will brown well, and it helps the floret to cook more quickly since it's thinner.

Once you're prepped, this is a quick one, so be sure the rest of your dinner is in the works before turning the burner on. I'd like some nice crispy chicken wings and legs with this, but this could be a great vegetarian entrée with some thick rice noodles.

1 TBSP OYSTER SAUCE	1 SMALL ONION (*4 to 5 oz/115 to 140 g*), *cut into 1-in/2.5-cm dice or wedges*
1½ TSP HOISIN SAUCE	KOSHER SALT
1 TSP SOY SAUCE	
1 TSP RICE WINE	6 OZ/170 G BROCCOLI FLORETS, *halved lengthwise*
¼ TSP CORNSTARCH	4 OZ/115 G CREMINI (*baby bella*) MUSHROOMS, *quartered*
2 TBSP PEANUT OIL	1 TBSP FINELY CHOPPED GARLIC

1 · *In a small bowl,* whisk together the oyster sauce, hoisin sauce, soy sauce, rice wine, 1 Tbsp of water, and the cornstarch.

2 · *In a large (12-in/30.5-cm) nonstick stir-fry pan,* heat the peanut oil over medium-high heat. Add the onion and a pinch of salt and turn the heat up to high. Cook, stirring, until the onion is broken up and the smaller pieces are just beginning to brown, about 2 minutes. Add the broccoli, the mushrooms, and a pinch of salt. Stir well. Cook, stirring only occasionally, until the vegetables are all shrunken and browned in spots, 8 to 10 minutes. Add the garlic and cook, stirring, until fragrant and just beginning to brown lightly, 30 to 40 seconds. Take the pan off the heat and let it rest for 30 seconds. Using a silicone spatula, stir well as you add the sauce. Continue to stir as the sauce thickens and coats the vegetables, 10 to 20 seconds. Immediately transfer the vegetables to a serving dish to prevent the sauce from scorching.

Serves 3

Stir-Fried Swiss Chard with Pine Nuts and Balsamic Butter

It may seem strange to stir-fry, rather than sauté, Swiss chard, but I think the stir-fry pan is handy for cooking both the stems and the leaves (as well as for browning the nuts). Often recipes will call for just the leaves of Swiss chard, but I think it's a shame to waste the stems. After separating them from the leaves, I slice the stems thinly. Then I cook them for about 5 minutes before adding the leaves, which only need a brief time in the pan. It makes me especially happy when those stems are the colorful orange, yellow, pink, and white ones of the Bright Lights variety of chard. I'm completely charmed by this colorful vegetable (which is now widely available), and I also like the slightly different flavors of the various colored leaves (yellow and orange are milder than red).

Chard can sometimes harbor a lot of grit, so unfortunately, you'll need to take the time to wash it well and spin the leaves dry before cooking (though you can do this ahead and store the leaves in zip-top bags). One thing about this dish, cooked chard begins to release liquid as it sits—this isn't a bad thing, as that liquid, enhanced with butter and balsamic, is delicious. It does mean, though, that I serve this in a bowl (either one large serving bowl or individual serving bowls) or with rice to soak up the liquid.

Like all greens, this dish would be delicious with polenta or a grain pilaf, but the deep, earthy flavors here would marry particularly well with a juicy steak.

1 TSP BALSAMIC VINEGAR	3 TBSP PINE NUTS
1 TSP SOY SAUCE	KOSHER SALT
½ TSP DARK BROWN SUGAR	2 TSP FINELY CHOPPED FRESH GARLIC
12 OZ/340 G BRIGHT LIGHTS SWISS CHARD (do not trim)	1 TBSP UNSALTED BUTTER
1 TBSP PEANUT OIL	

1   *In a small bowl,* combine the balsamic vinegar, soy sauce, and brown sugar.

2   *Pull or cut the stems away* from the chard leaves. Cut or rip the leaves into 2- to 3-in/ 5- to 7.5-cm pieces and wash and dry them well. Rinse the stems and slice them crosswise into ¼-in/6.5-mm pieces.

{ Continued }

3   *Heat the peanut oil* in a large (12 in/30.5 cm) nonstick stir-fry pan over medium heat. When the oil is hot (it will loosen and spread out), add the pine nuts and cook, stirring almost constantly, until they're all lightly browned, 1 to 2 minutes. Watch carefully, because they brown quickly. Remove the pan from the heat and use a slotted spoon or spatula to transfer the pine nuts to a heat-proof plate or pan, leaving behind as much fat as possible.

4   *Return the pan to the heat,* add the chard stems and a pinch of salt, and cook, stirring occasionally, until they're shrunken and beginning to brown lightly, about 5 minutes. (They will begin to crackle in the pan as moisture evaporates.) Add the garlic and stir-fry just until fragrant, a few seconds. Add the chard leaves and ½ tsp salt and, using tongs, toss the chard leaves in the pan just until wilted (30 to 45 seconds). Scrape the balsamic mixture into the pan, stir, and remove the pan from the heat. Add the butter and toss and stir until it's melted. Fold in half of the pine nuts. Transfer the chard (including all of the stems and liquid) to a small serving bowl and garnish with the remaining pine nuts.

Serves 2 to 3

Chapter 10
Grilling

METHOD: Grilling

EQUIPMENT: Gas grill, long-handled tongs, metal grill basket, trays or sheet pans, mixing bowls, foil

HEAT: The gas grill, cranked up

....

Grilling: How It Works

You've got to love the grill. Once I cooked an entire meal on mine in the middle of a hurricane, because the electricity had gone out and I had a huge family gathering on my hands. I stood outside in my foul-weather gear and had a dandy time, even managing to find a spot on the grill to finish baking a vegetable gratin (it was delicious). But even under ordinary circumstances, I love how easy and fast the grill is, and that I don't have to wash a pot or pan.

By grill, of course, I'm talking about a gas grill. I learned to grill on hardwood charcoal, and I still love it, but for speed and convenience (two things we care about in this book), the gas grill is it. Also, the slightly gentler, more moist heat of the gas grill is kinder to vegetables. And I like that, because I want you to get friendly with grilling vegetables. Over the years, a lot of folks have told me they get stuck in a grilling rut—all chicken breasts and hamburgers, all the time. Learning to cook a variety of vegetables on the grill will not only give you one more convenient weeknight vegetable-cooking technique, but it will also liven up your repertoire, including your entertaining menus.

Okay, here's the skinny on grilling vegetables:

- First, get to know your grill. All grills have their own personality. Get to know where the hot spots are and just how hot the grill is when your knob is pointing to medium-high. One grill's medium-high is another grill's medium, which is why you might have to make slight adjustments to the timing in these recipes after making them once or twice. They've all been tested on at least two different grills, but yours may still run much hotter or cooler. When cooking a recipe for the first time, make a note in the book or on a piece of paper if, for instance, your zucchini slices aren't well marked in 3 to 4 minutes on your medium-hot grill.

- Keep in mind that gas grills function best when covered. The lid allows the hot air that's being generated at the burner level to convect all around the inside of the grill, helping food to cook evenly. Even though you will be cooking the vegetables in this chapter over direct heat (as opposed to indirect heat with a burner turned off), the vegetables will still benefit from hot air circulating around them.

- Be prepared before you start grilling. Have a grilling kit ready: good spring-loaded, long-handled tongs (I like Oxo's), sheet pans on which to spread out sliced vegetables, a timer, an old dish towel or pot holder for handling hot stuff, a good wire-bristled brush for cleaning the grill before you start, and a grill basket (see below).

- For some veggies, a grill basket works best. These handy wok- or bowl-shaped containers are available in most housewares and kitchen stores. Cooking in one is a little like having your stir fry pan on the grill. The baskets allow you to cook vegetables like green beans) that would otherwise fall through the cracks.

- Give your veggies their best shot. Slice or cut vegetables on the diagonal (so they're longer and won't fall through the grates) and to a thickness (often between ⅜ and ½ inch/9.5 mm and 1.25 cm) that will cook through in the same amount of time it takes to brown both sides. If you cut veggies too thick, they will still be unpleasantly raw on the inside when the outsides look done.

- Remember this trick for finishing vegetables (especially large mushrooms, onions, and eggplant) off the grill: Stack and wrap them in foil and let the residual heat cook them through. Grilled vegetables are not going to be crisp anyway, and the moist heat of the foil package simply allows for a much more tender, pleasant texture.

- No matter how you cook the veggies, make sure they're well coated with olive oil. My grilling-guru friend Elizabeth Karmel puts hers in a zip-top bag to mix them with the oil—a great idea. I use one of my stainless-steel mixing bowls. Don't worry if it looks like a lot of oil going on. Just toss the vegetables well and lift them out of the bowl; excess oil will be left behind. (And you can use that to toss with another veggie.) The purpose of the oil is to carry the heat around and through the vegetable. Without it, you will have a dry, undercooked, crispy critter.

Now to the good stuff—the recipes. In this chapter, you'll learn a great way to grill corn on the cob, how to make delicious grilled potatoes, and how to turn grilled peppers into lovely salads or starters. You'll also get recipes for grilling some more unusual vegetables, like broccoli rabe. Last (or first), this chapter presents you with a chart of grilling times and cuts for some popular vegetables, so you can improvise on a weeknight, if you like, or put together a platter for a party.

VEGETABLES FOR GRILLING

VEGETABLE	WAY TO CUT	QUANTITY OIL PER 12 OZ/340 G	GRILL TEMPERATURE	COOKING TIME
Asparagus	tough ends removed	2 tsp	high	1 minute per side
Bell peppers	uncut; peel after cooking	no oil	high	2 to 3 minutes per side to blister all over
Eggplant	skin scored with fork, sliced ⅜ in/9.5 mm thick	2 to 3 Tbsp	medium-high	4 to 6 minutes per side
Mushrooms, cremini (baby bella)	stems trimmed	2 to 3 Tbsp	medium	5 to 7 minutes per side
Mushrooms, portabella	stems and gills removed	2 to 3 Tbsp	high	5 to 8 minutes first side, 2 to 3 minutes second side
Mushrooms, shiitake	stems removed	2 Tbsp	medium	3 to 4 minutes first side, 2 to 3 minutes second side
Onions, red or yellow	peeled, sliced ½ in/1.25 cm thick, and threaded on skewers or turkey lacers	2 Tbsp	medium	6 to 7 minutes per side
Potatoes, baby red or yellow	halved and boiled until tender	3 Tbsp	medium	3 to 5 minutes first side, 2 to 3 minutes second side
Tomatoes, plum	halved and seeded	2 to 3 Tbsp	medium, then low	6 to 8 minutes, cut side down, on medium, 8 to 10 minutes, skin side down, on low
Zucchini and summer squash	ends trimmed, sliced ⅜ in/9.5 mm thick on the diagonal	1 to 2 Tbsp	medium-high	3 to 4 minutes first side, 2 to 4 minutes second side

Foundation Recipe for Grilling

I can't tell you how many times I've put out a platter of grilled vegetables for a party, or taken one to a potluck, only to see them disappear before anyone digs into the potato salad nearby. People love grilled vegetables. This foundation recipe will allow you to assemble one of these platters, if you like, or it will just help you grill one of your favorite vegetables on a weeknight.

The key to this recipe is the table on page 174. The table provides prepping directions, temperatures, and approximate times for grilling ten popular vegetables. To keep things simple, all of these vegetables are ones that cook best directly on the grate. For vegetables like beans and broccoli raab that benefit from the grill basket, follow the recipes on page 177 and page 187. I've included plum tomatoes in the chart, though I have to caution you that grilling tomatoes takes some getting used to, and they have their own karma. Relatively firm plum tomatoes that have been seeded will brown up nicely if cooked, cut side down, for several minutes. Then, when flipped over and moved to low heat, they will give off a lot of their remaining moisture and become very tasty. Sometimes, however, they just plain stick and fall apart, so cook them when you have a little time to mess around and not a lot of guests coming over.

Since there are so many sauces and flavor boosts in the other recipes in this chapter, I have kept the finishing flourish simple. (You can certainly steal something like the Thyme-Dijon Butter on page 177 or the Creamy Lemon Dressing on page 182, or you can drizzle your favorite vinaigrette over the vegetables.) But I think for a simple side dish—especially for a buffet or potluck—a drizzle of olive oil and a squeeze of lemon is sometimes the best way to enjoy that intense grilled flavor. I am not big on marinating vegetables (with the exception of mushrooms) before grilling. I think marinades can sometimes overpower the flavor of grilled summer vegetables or adversely affect the cooking, so I usually add flavor boosts afterward.

The directions here are for grilling just one type of vegetable. Depending on your grill and the vegetables you choose, you might be able to do two or more types of vegetables at the same time. And you can certainly do one right after the other, because grilled vegetables are great at room temperature. You do not have to do them to order (!) and you can cook them ahead.

{ Continued }

For a party, have fun with the presentation. I like to use a big white platter, and starting at one end, I arrange sections of grilled zucchini, grilled peppers, grilled asparagus, grilled mushrooms, and grilled onions. After a drizzle of oil and lemon, I often garnish with both chopped fresh herbs and a few pretty herb sprigs. You could put lemon or lime wedges on the platter, too.

12 OZ/340 G YOUR CHOICE OF VEGETABLE *(see the table on page 174 for choices and how to cut them)*

¼ TO ½ TSP KOSHER SALT

EXTRA-VIRGIN OLIVE OIL *for coating and drizzling*

¼ LEMON OR LIME

2 TSP CHOPPED OR TORN FRESH PARSLEY, MINT, BASIL, CILANTRO, OR TARRAGON; *or 1 tsp whole fresh thyme or oregano leaves*

1 *After choosing your vegetable,* preheat a gas grill to the temperature indicated in the table. Put a sheet pan or a platter next to the grill, so that you'll have some place to put the vegetables as they come off the grill (some will cook faster than others). Make sure your tongs are handy, too.

2 *Prep the vegetable* as indicated in the table. In a medium mixing bowl, toss the vegetable thoroughly with ¼ to ½ tsp kosher salt and the amount of olive oil called for in the chart. (Some vegetables, like eggplant, need more. Whole bell peppers, on the other hand, need none.) Alternatively, if the vegetables are sliced (like zucchini and eggplant), lay them out on a sheet pan and brush the oil on so that you don't risk some slices soaking up more oil than others.

3 *When the grill is hot,* use a wire grill brush to clean the grates. Arrange the vegetables, evenly spaced, directly on the grate and close the lid. Set a timer for the minimum grilling time given in the table. Open the lid, and check the undersides of the vegetables to see if they're browned or marked. If so, use tongs to carefully turn them over. Then close the lid again. If they're not well marked, continue cooking for another minute or two, check again, and flip. Transfer the vegetables to the sheet pan or platter as they finish cooking. (Don't stack high-moisture vegetables like zucchini, as they'll overcook. Vegetables that may need more interior cooking, like eggplant, onions, and mushrooms, can be stacked and even wrapped in foil to finish cooking.) Because of hot and cool spots on the grill, vegetables will cook at different rates, so you will want to move some vegetables around if they're stuck in cool spots.

4 *When all of the vegetables are cooked,* arrange them on a serving dish. (Whole peppers will need to be peeled and sliced first.) Drizzle a little olive oil and squeeze a bit of lemon over them. Garnish with the fresh herbs.

Serves 3 to 4

Grilled Green Beans with Thyme-Dijon Butter

Yes, it's true that grilled green beans are not the prettiest thing to look at, but they are really tasty, and they're also an unexpected (and easy) preparation for a popular vegetable. This is one of the times when you'll be really happy to have a grill basket on hand, as there's no other good way to grill green beans (without losing most of them through the grates).

Once the grill basket is good and hot, all you need do is toss the beans in and stir (with tongs) from time to time. The more you stir, the more evenly they'll cook. But since opening and closing the grill lid a lot releases heat, don't stir them too, too much. It's fine if some of them are darker than others. (The smaller ones will cook faster.)

You can serve the beans plain, but I especially like them with Thyme-Dijon Butter, flavored with mustard, lemon, capers, and thyme. Double it if you like. It keeps for a week in the fridge and is good on grilled meat as well as vegetables. Or feel free to substitute a flavored butter on page 29.

These beans would be nice with grilled chicken thighs and an arugula salad.

Thyme-Dijon Butter

2 TBSP UNSALTED BUTTER, *well softened*

1 TSP DIJON MUSTARD

1 TSP CHOPPED FRESH THYME

1 TSP MINCED DRAINED CAPERS

½ TSP FINELY GRATED LEMON ZEST

⅛ TSP KOSHER SALT

12 OZ/340 G GREEN BEANS, *trimmed*

1 TBSP EXTRA-VIRGIN OLIVE OIL

¼ TSP KOSHER SALT, *and more if needed*

FLOWERING THYME SPRIGS OR LEMON WEDGES *for garnish (optional)*

1. *To make the Thyme-Dijon Butter:* combine the butter, mustard, thyme, capers, lemon zest, and salt in a small bowl and mash together with a small spatula or a spoon. Refrigerate until using.

2. *Put a grill basket* directly on the grate of your gas grill and heat the grill to medium-high. When the grill and the basket are hot, toss the green beans with the olive oil and ¼ tsp salt. Put them in the grill basket, toss, cover the grill, and cook, tossing the beans every couple of minutes with tongs, until all of the beans are limp and blackened in places (smaller ones will be very dark), 8 to 9 minutes.

3. *Transfer the beans* to a mixing bowl (or a shallow serving bowl) and toss with 1 Tbsp Thyme-Dijon Butter (or more if you like) until the butter has melted and coated the beans. Taste and add more salt if necessary. Serve with thyme sprigs or lemon wedges as a garnish, if desired.

Serves 3

Grill-Roasted Bell Peppers with Goat Cheese and Cherry Tomato Dressing

If you're a fan of roasted peppers, you'll be happy to know that you can roast them on your grill. The high heat that circulates around the pepper actually does a better job of blistering than the broiler, and it only takes about 10 minutes. Then all you have to do is steam the peppers in foil for 5 to 10 minutes, until they're cool enough to peel.

I like to take advantage of how delicious the peppers are when they're still warm, so I cut them in half, fill them with a bit of softened goat cheese, and spoon a beautiful cherry tomato dressing over the top. (Depending on how well your peppers hold together after roasting, I've given you two options for serving them; both are pretty.) Sure, this makes a nice side dish, but served on individual salad plates, it also makes a lovely starter for a summer gathering of friends. If you're not crazy about goat cheese, you could substitute fresh ricotta.

3 BELL PEPPERS OF UNIFORM SIZE (*try mixing red, orange, and yellow*)

3 OZ/85 G FRESH GOAT CHEESE, *at room temperature*

1 RECIPE SUMMER CHERRY TOMATO DRESSING (*facing page*)

6 SMALL SPRIGS FRESH BASIL

1   *Preheat a gas grill to high.* Put the whole bell peppers directly on the grate, lower the lid, and cook, turning with tongs every couple of minutes, until the peppers are well blistered and blackened in places, about 10 minutes. (Blistering is enough to release the skin—don't completely blacken all over or the skin will begin to stick to the pepper.) Transfer the peppers to a bowl and cover with foil. (Or wrap the peppers loosely in foil.) Let sit for 8 to 10 minutes. Over a sink or a bowl, peel the skin away from the peppers; it should come right off. Leaving the stems in, cut the peppers in half. Gently remove the seeds, but keep any accumulated liquid inside if you can (it has lots of flavor).

2   *Depending on how intact* your pepper halves are, you have two choices for serving them: If they're still cup-shaped, leave the stem end in. If they are somewhat flattened or torn, go ahead and remove the stem and the flesh clinging to it and let the pepper lie flat. Arrange the pepper halves on six salad plates. Spoon ½ oz/15 g goat cheese into or on each pepper half. Flatten the cheese and spread it out just a little (leave it somewhat mounded). If the pepper half is flat, fold one side of it over to enclose the cheese, ravioli-style (on the diagonal) and gently press down on it to flatten the cheese a bit. Spoon an equal portion of the tomato dressing over each of the six pepper halves, crossing from one side of the plate to the other. Garnish each with a small basil sprig.

Serves 6

SUMMER CHERRY TOMATO DRESSING

This lovely dressing is really more like a fresh compote or a loose salsa. It's the place to use your tiniest, prettiest, most colorful tomatoes (and not those large, tough cherry tomatoes from the grocery store). While this is delicious paired with the Grill-Roasted Bell Peppers on page 178, it's also good over grilled eggplant and grilled skirt steak.

8 OZ/225 G SMALL CHERRY OR OTHER TINY TOMATOES, *halved or quartered, depending on size*

3 TBSP EXTRA-VIRGIN OLIVE OIL

2 TBSP THINLY SLICED DRAINED OIL-PACKED SUN-DRIED TOMATOES

1 TBSP THINLY SLICED FRESH BASIL LEAVES

2 TSP DRAINED CAPERS, *coarsely chopped*

2 TSP SHERRY VINEGAR

2 TSP FRESH ORANGE JUICE

½ TSP MINCED FRESH GARLIC

¼ TSP KOSHER SALT

1 *Combine all of the ingredients* in a small bowl and stir gently to combine. Let sit for 10 to 15 minutes (or up to 30 minutes) to let the flavors mingle and to let the tomatoes marinate a bit. Stir gently again before serving.

Yields about 1¼ cups/300 ml

Sesame-Ginger Marinated Grilled Shiitakes

I always pop a few of these yummy mushrooms in my mouth before I even get them into the house. If enough survive, I add them to a platter of grilled vegetables, toss them into a spinach or mizuna salad, or serve them with grilled skirt steak or shrimp. They're also good in a steak sandwich.

I keep the marinade very simple for these, so there's nothing subtle about the flavor (as if shiitakes were shy, anyway!). My method for marinating the mushrooms is a little unusual. I lay out the caps and spoon the marinade on top of them. I find this is best for getting the flavor where it needs to go without having to make a lot of marinade. One bit of advice—if at all possible, buy your shiitakes from a bulk bin, so that you can pick out the biggest ones. Large or medium caps are fine for grilling, but the little ones tend to fall through the cracks (though if they survive, they still taste good!).

The marinating time in this recipe is short, so heat your grill while you're prepping, and you'll soon have a quick side dish or salad ingredient.

8 TO 9 OZ/225 TO 255 G LARGE SHIITAKE MUSHROOMS, *stemmed* *(yielding 6 to 7 oz/170 to 200 g)*

2 TBSP LOW-SODIUM SOY SAUCE

1 TBSP PEANUT OIL

1 TBSP SESAME OIL

1 TBSP RICE WINE

1 TBSP CHOPPED FRESH GINGER

1 *Preheat a gas grill* to medium.

2 *In a shallow dish,* such as a medium-size baking dish, arrange the mushroom caps in one layer, stem side up. In a small bowl, whisk together the soy sauce, peanut oil, sesame oil, rice wine, and ginger. With a small spoon (like a ½-tsp measure), spoon some marinade over each cap, distributing the marinade as evenly as possible. Let sit for 10 minutes, and then toss to coat the cap side before grilling.

3 *Arrange the caps,* stem side up, directly on the grill grate. Drizzle any leftover marinade on top of them if you like. Cover and cook until the caps are darkened or well marked on the bottom, 3 to 4 minutes. Turn over and cook just until the other side is marked, 2 to 3 minutes. Serve these right away on their own or use them as an ingredient in a salad or sandwich.

Serves 3 to 4

Grilled Baby Potatoes with Creamy Lemon Dressing

I make grilled potatoes just about every way you can, but none of the techniques are super-fast. Nevertheless, I wanted to include a recipe for them in the book, because my friends love these and always ask for the recipe. This technique has a make-ahead component to it, making it easier to adapt the recipe to your schedule.

This is what I do: I boil the potatoes first until they're tender. (That's the part you could do ahead, say, in the morning, and refrigerate them until you're ready to grill in the evening.) Then I toss them in a mixture of mayonnaise and mustard (and plenty of salt) and grill them until they're brown and crusty on the outside, which only takes about 5 minutes. Because they've been boiled first, they have a fluffy texture on the inside. Plus, they're not on the grill for too long, so they don't have a chance to dry out. The mayo coating also keeps moisture in.

The bottom line is that these are really yummy, and you can eat them plain or dress them up with a vinaigrette and a few salad greens (or even add them to a composed salad). Here, I've included a delicious and quickly made Creamy Lemon Dressing to serve with them. (You can make it while the potatoes are cooking.) What starts out as a very lemony vinaigrette becomes smooth and a little bit creamy when a bit of mayonnaise is mixed in. You can dip the potatoes into the dressing or spoon it on, whatever the occasion calls for.

Creamy Lemon Dressing	1 LB/455 G RED OR YELLOW BABY POTATOES *(about 1½ in/3.75 cm in diameter)*, halved
2 TBSP EXTRA-VIRGIN OLIVE OIL	
½ TSP FINELY GRATED LEMON ZEST	2¾ TSP KOSHER SALT
2 TSP FRESH LEMON JUICE	¼ CUP/55 G MAYONNAISE
½ TSP DIJON MUSTARD	1 TBSP DIJON MUSTARD
¼ TSP SUGAR	1 TSP FRESH LEMON JUICE
⅛ TSP KOSHER SALT	
1 TO 2 TSP MAYONNAISE	

1   *To make the Creamy Lemon Dressing:* combine the olive oil, lemon zest, lemon juice, ½ tsp mustard, sugar, and salt in a small bowl and whisk thoroughly until well combined and emulsified. Whisk in the 1 to 2 tsp mayonnaise until it's completely smooth. (If you like a thicker and less tangy dressing, put in all of the mayo.) If making ahead, refrigerate until ready to serve. You may need to rewhisk the dressing just before serving.

2   *Before starting the potatoes,* arrange a few layers of dish towels on a baking sheet to drain them. Put the potatoes and 2 tsp of the salt in a large saucepan and cover with water by at least 1 in/2.5 cm. Bring to a boil, reduce to a simmer, and cook until just tender, 20 to 25 minutes. Drain and rinse lightly with cool water. Spread the potatoes out on the prepared baking sheet and refrigerate them for at least 10 minutes and up to 10 hours to cool down. (Alternatively, let them cool at room temperature.)

3   *Preheat a gas grill* to medium (not medium-high).

4   *In a mixing bowl* big enough to hold the potatoes, whisk together the ¼ cup/55g mayonnaise, 1 Tbsp mustard, and lemon juice.

5   *Put the cooled potatoes* in the bowl with the mayo mixture and sprinkle the remaining ¾ tsp salt over them. Use a silicone spatula to gently toss and coat them with the mayo mixture. Using tongs, arrange the potatoes, cut side down, on the hot grill grate. Put the lid down and cook until that side is nicely marked or brown, 3 to 5 minutes. Flip the potatoes over and cook the skin side until it's browned, 2 to 3 minutes more. Put the Creamy Lemon Dressing in a small bowl and put it on a serving platter. Transfer the potatoes to the platter.

Serves 3 to 4

Grilled Asparagus with Grilled Prosciutto, Lemon, and Parmigiano

In less than 5 minutes the components for this dish go on and off the grill. The prosciutto only needs about a minute to crisp up, and the asparagus only 2 minutes (I use high heat). The grilled lemons are mostly for garnish, though sliced paper thin, they're perfectly edible and many people like them.

Because of the quick grilling time, you won't want to wander away from the grill. You can bring your handy timer with you, but because things happen so fast (you flip the prosciutto after about 30 seconds and the asparagus after about a minute), you might have to rely on eyeballing. Look for the prosciutto to shrink and crisp up and the asparagus to be nicely marked on the bottom. The lemon slices can hang out while you're doing all this, as they take a bit longer.

This is a very antipasto-like dish, so serve it as a first course if you like, or alongside grilled fish. This dish is pretty in a rustic kind of way, and the right plates make a difference.

16 THIN ASPARAGUS SPEARS, *trimmed*

2 TSP EXTRA-VIRGIN OLIVE OIL, *and more for drizzling (or use walnut or hazelnut oil for drizzling)*

¼ TSP KOSHER SALT

1 LEMON, *halved crosswise*

4 THIN *(but not ultrathin)* **SLICES PROSCIUTTO DI PARMA**

SEA SALT

WEDGE OF PARMIGIANO-REGGIANO

FRESHLY GROUND BLACK PEPPER

1   *Preheat a gas grill to high.* Toss the asparagus with the 2 tsp olive oil and the kosher salt. Cut 4 paper-thin slices from one of the lemon halves. Reserve the other half for seasoning at the end.

2   *Arrange the asparagus,* lemon slices, and prosciutto slices, on the grill and close the lid. Cook until everything is well marked on the bottom, 30 seconds for the prosciutto, and about 1 minute for the asparagus and the lemon slices. Turn over each item, close the lid again, and continue cooking. When the prosciutto is crisp, about 30 seconds more, remove it from the grill. Grill the asparagus just until marked on the second side, about 1 minute more, or a total of 2 minutes. Grill the lemon slices until they're very well browned, 1 to 2 minutes more, for a total of 2 to 3 minutes. Remove the asparagus and lemon slices from the grill.

3   *On each of four antipasto or salad plates* (or on the side of four dinner plates), arrange four asparagus spears. Squeeze some juice from the lemon half over all, and sprinkle on a few grains of sea salt. Using a Y-shaped vegetable peeler, slice four or five large, wide curls (or shavings) of Parmigiano-Reggiano over the asparagus. Top with a prosciutto crisp and a lemon slice, and drizzle a bit of oil back and forth over all. Season with a few grinds of pepper over and around the asparagus.

Serves 4

Foil-Grilled Corn on the Cob with Maple Butter

I love this method of grilling corn, because it's mostly hands-off and it yields corn that's both juicy and toasty tasting. I shuck the corn and rub it all over with butter. Then I wrap it, along with a few herb sprigs, in foil. The corn goes directly on the grill grate for 15 to 20 minutes (you'll need to turn it every few minutes). Inside, the corn kernels steam, and they also get yummy patches of browning from the butter.

I've served this corn with a lot of different flavored butters, but I think Maple Butter is the most delicious. It tastes like great pancakes for dinner. Kids love this, but if you're looking for a slightly more sophisticated flavor, the addition of lime zest to the Maple Butter is just the thing. (Either way, be sure the butter is well-softened before mixing in the maple or it will not incorporate.)

Obviously, you can double or triple this recipe if you like. It would be great with barbecued chicken and the New Potato Salad with Fresh Peas, Lime, and Yogurt (page 133) on the Fourth of July.

Maple Butter	4 EARS CORN, SHUCKED, *silks removed*
3 TBSP UNSALTED BUTTER, *softened*	4 TSP UNSALTED BUTTER
2 TSP PURE MAPLE SYRUP	KOSHER SALT
⅛ TSP KOSHER SALT	FRESHLY GROUND BLACK PEPPER
½ TSP FINELY GRATED LIME ZEST *(optional)*	12 TO 16 SPRIGS FRESH THYME

1   *To make the Maple Butter:* combine the 3 Tbsp butter, maple syrup, ⅛ tsp salt, and lime zest in a small bowl and mix well with a rubber spatula. Set aside.

2   *Preheat a gas grill to medium-high.* Arrange four sheets of foil (about 12-in/30.5-cm square) on your counter. Rub each ear of corn all over with 1 tsp of the butter (you can use a little less if you like). Season the corn with salt and pepper and tuck 3 or 4 herb sprigs around each ear. Roll each ear up tightly in its foil wrapper (tuck the ends of the foil in as you go).

3   *Put the ears of corn* directly on the grill grate. Grill for 15 to 18 minutes, rolling each ear of corn over (about a quarter turn) every 5 or 6 minutes so that each side of the corn eventually has direct contact with the grate. Unroll a little of the foil and take a peek at each ear, which should have some browning patches. If it doesn't, rewrap the ear and put it back on the grill (in one of the hottest spots) until browned in places, about 5 minutes more.

4   *Remove the corn* from the grill and carefully loosen the foil around each ear. Let sit for a few minutes and serve with the Maple Butter for spreading.

Serves 4

Grilled Broccoli Rabe with Lemon and Parmigiano

I first tried grilling broccoli rabe after reading in *The Zuni Café Cookbook* how chef Judy Rodgers does it; she tosses the rabe in both water and oil before grilling. This is ingenious, because the water helps the tough rabe stems steam while the leaves and florets caramelize. My method varies a bit from hers in that I've found that using a grill basket helps to cook the rabe a little more thoroughly than spreading it out on the grate. The leaves don't get quite as crisp, but the stems cook more evenly. I also like to cut the thickest stems in half lengthwise first.

I think a simple finish of a little lemon and Parmigiano is all this quick and easy vegetable dish needs. If you're a rabe fan, you've got to try grilling it—you'll love it. If you haven't tried rabe or are serving it to friends, I recommend trying it boiled first (see cooking times, page 116), as boiling makes the raab milder when grilled. Be generous with the Parmigiano and serve the rabe with a simple flatbread or grilled pizza.

8 OZ/225 G BROCCOLI RABE, *bottom 2 in/ 5 cm of stems trimmed, all stems but the very thinnest cut in half lengthwise*

3 TBSP EXTRA-VIRGIN OLIVE OIL

KOSHER SALT

¼ LEMON

SMALL WEDGE OF PARMIGIANO-REGGIANO

1   *Put a vegetable grilling basket* directly on the grate of a gas grill and preheat it to medium. When the grill and the basket are hot, toss the broccoli rabe in a mixing bowl with the olive oil, 3 Tbsp water, and ½ tsp salt, and transfer it to the grill basket. Toss well, close the lid, and cook, tossing frequently with tongs (and reclosing the lid each time), until the rabe is wilted and all of the pieces have some browning on them, 7 to 8 minutes.

2   *Transfer the rabe* to a serving platter. Taste and add a little salt if necessary. Season with a light squeeze of the lemon, and, using a Y-shaped vegetable peeler, shave as many Parmigiano shavings as you like (8 to 10 would be good) over the rabe. Serve warm or at room temperature.

Serves 3 to 4

Grilled Eggplant "Sandwiches" with Goat Cheese, Sun-Dried Tomatoes, and Fresh Herbs

Over the years, I've made lots of versions of these grilled eggplant sandwiches, and everyone loves them. You can tuck a few into a spinach or arugula salad or serve them with grilled lamb. Remember one tip about grilling eggplant: It browns up fairly quickly on the outside, and tends not to cook through. The best solution to this problem is, after removing the slices from the grill, to stack and wrap them in a foil pouch for 10 or 15 minutes, and the residual heat will finish cooking them. The flesh will be tender and silky, as it should be. Eggplant skin doesn't bother me, but if it annoys you, score the skin with a fork before slicing or use a vegetable peeler to peel away alternating lengthwise strips of skin. Leaving some skin will help hold the slices together after cooking.

1 LB/455 G ITALIAN EGGPLANT (*about 2*)

3 TBSP EXTRA-VIRGIN OLIVE OIL

½ TSP PLUS ⅛ TSP KOSHER SALT

4 OZ/115 G FRESH GOAT CHEESE, *at room temperature*

2 TBSP ORANGE JUICE

2 TBSP CHOPPED DRAINED OIL-PACKED SUN-DRIED TOMATOES

ABOUT 20 SMALL FRESH BASIL AND/OR MINT LEAVES

1 *Preheat a gas grill to medium-high.* Trim the ends of the eggplant and slice it across into ⅜-in/9.5-mm slices. (You will have about 20 to 24 slices). Arrange the slices on a baking sheet and brush both sides with the olive oil. Sprinkle the ½ tsp salt over both sides, too.

2 *Put the slices directly on the grill,* close the lid, and cook until nicely marked or browned on both sides, 4 to 6 minutes per side. Transfer the eggplant to a plate or tray and arrange the slices in stacks of 4 or 5 slices close together. Cover the plate with aluminum foil (or wrap the stacks in a foil pouch). Let sit for 10 to 15 minutes. The eggplant will finish cooking through.

3 *Meanwhile, in a small bowl,* combine the goat cheese, orange juice, sun-dried tomatoes, and the ⅛ tsp salt. Mash together until thoroughly combined.

4 *Unwrap the eggplant* and arrange half of the slices (choose the biggest ones for the bottom of the sandwich) on a board or tray. Spoon some of the goat cheese mixture on each slice. Top each with two herb leaves and another eggplant slice.

Yields 10 to 12 sandwiches; serves 4

Chapter 11
Baking
Gratins

(Bonus Chapter—Slower but Worth It)

METHOD: Baking gratins

EQUIPMENT: Shallow baking dishes in 2-cup/475-ml, 5- to 6-cup/1.2- to 1.4-L, and 2-qt/2-L sizes

HEAT: A moderate oven

···

Baking Gratins: How It Works

"It's just a casserole, really," I said to my friend Ali when I brought a gratin to a family supper at her house one night not long after I met her. She remembers that well, because she was so happy to discover that a former editor of a national cooking magazine wasn't pretentious about food. I didn't try to impress her with something fussy, but it turns out that I did bring a dish with a name that's hard to pronounce. Because of my French culinary training, I use the French pronunciation for gratin (grah-TAHN), a cheese-and-crumb-topped layered vegetable dish. But it's okay if you want to use the English pronunciation (GROT-ten). After all, it's just a casserole.

I should add that it's a shallow casserole. (This is not a deep-dish affair.) One of the reasons a gratin is so tasty is that the contents of the dish are spread out over a surface area that's relatively large compared to their volume. That means that lots of vegetables get to make contact with the pan, so you have more of the delicious browned, caramelized stuff. Plus, all that surface area means that juices and liquids can bubble away. While they reduce and thicken, they also get more flavorful.

So, do you need a special gratin dish? No, both Pyrex and Corning make shallow baking dishes that work fine. But there are two reasons why you might *want* a special gratin dish: material and looks. I really like my 2-qt/2-L Le Creuset enameled cast-iron oval gratin dish because it conducts heat so well. I also like my Pillivuyt 5-cup/1.2-L white ceramic gratin dish, because its simple good looks show off the contents of a gratin beautifully. And since gratins take a little time and effort to put together (yes, this is the bonus "slower-but-worth it" chapter), you'll want to make them to share at potlucks and serve at parties.

You'll also want to have a couple of different-size dishes on hand if you like making gratins. Most of the recipes in this chapter call for one of the following: a 2-qt/2-L shallow baking dish (Pyrex makes a rectangular one), which serves about six people; a 5- to 6-cup/1.2- to 1.4-L shallow baking dish (you can use a Pyrex 9½-in/24-cm pie dish in a pinch), which serves four people; and a mini–gratin dish, which serves one or two. Look for a mini with a volume of between 2 and 2½ cups/475 and 590 ml. (They are usually about 8 in/20 cm long.) They're not hard to find in housewares or kitchen stores, and Emile Henry and Le Creuset make pretty ones. All of these dishes should have a depth of no more than 1½ to 2 in/3.75 to 5 cm. They can be oval, rectangular, or even round—as long as they are shallow.

I wish I had room in this book to tell you about all the different kinds of gratins you can make, but since this is a bonus chapter, I've narrowed my offerings to two main types of gratins (and a couple of ringers). The first is a potato-based gratin. These classic casseroles are so hearty and delicious that I've given you a template for one in the foundation recipe. Those gratins are satisfying on chilly nights. But the other style of gratin that I like to make a lot works best in summer. The French also lay claim to inventing this dish, which is called a *tian*. It's a much lighter kind of gratin, with rows of tomatoes and other summer vegetables arranged over a bed of onions, seasoned with fresh herbs, and topped, of course, with a bit of cheese and bread crumbs. With the long, slow cooking, juices from the vegetables cook down into a delicious elixir. Then there are a couple of gratins in this chapter that showcase leafy greens and butternut squash.

But back to those bread crumbs for a minute. I don't use crusty artisan bread for these; I really like English muffins. I buy them by the bagful, rip them up, and pulse them in my food processor (or in my coffee grinder if it's just one muffin). I like the texture of these crumbs for a more substantial crust. Plus, the muffins are easy to dispatch. Sometimes I'll use pita breads to make finer crumbs. Either way, I try to make the crumbs in batches and store them in zip-top bags in my freezer so that they're at the ready when I need them.

Well, instead of continuing to expound about the finer points of gratins, I think I'd better release you to find out how delicious they are yourself. Remember to set aside a bit of time for prep; once you get these in the oven, you can cozy up with your tea or wine and just inhale the wonderful aromas wafting from your kitchen.

Foundation Recipe for Baking Gratins

There are zillions of different kinds of potato gratins in the world, but the classic is the French dish of potatoes, Gruyère cheese, and cream known as potatoes dauphinoise. In the States, we call a very similar dish potatoes au gratin or scalloped potatoes. And I just call mine a potato gratin. My version comes very close to the classic French dish, except that I have cut the cream with some chicken broth. And, of course, since this is a foundation recipe, I've created some opportunities (but not too many) for you to customize your dish. I decided to limit the options, because I didn't want to overwhelm you if you've never made one of these before. I also want you to experience this at its best, because it's a classic for a reason. But once you've made a potato–Gruyère cheese version, you can try out some different combos.

I think varying the cheese is the place to have fun here. I made one recently with half Swiss cheese and half aged Gouda, and it was so flavorful. Nutty Gruyère is hard to beat, but other good melting cheeses like Fontina and Emmental are nice, too. When I use hard aged cheeses like Parmigiano and aged Gouda, they make up no more than half of the total amount of cheese; used alone they wouldn't provide the unctuous texture that the others do.

If you like, you can replace half of the Yukon gold potatoes with either sweet potato or celery root. I like the celery root version a lot, as the creamy gratin lets just enough of this root vegetable's distinctive flavor come through. You'll also have a chance to vary flavors with your choice of herbs or an addition of ham or bacon.

For this and other gratins, you'll need to slice the potatoes or other root vegetables thinly. Unlike some cooks, I don't use a mandoline for this job. I find that both my Santoku knife and my ceramic knife work beautifully for creating very thin slices (ideally, between 1⁄16 and 1⁄8 in/1.5 and 3.25 mm). Japanese-style chef's knives or any sharp knife with a thin blade would work, too. So that I'm not cutting a wobbly round shape, I always cut the vegetable in half lengthwise first. Then I can put the halves, cut side down, flat against the cutting board for stability. But if you're more comfortable with a mandoline, go ahead and use it. Just be sure to use the guard!

Once you've grated your cheese, chopped some herbs, and sliced some potatoes, all you need do is mix them together and pour them into the dish. This recipe, which serves four people, is designed to be a manageable size and not just a special-occasion dish. With only 1 lb/455 g of potatoes to slice, the prep isn't too time-consuming. If you don't have a shallow 5- or 6-cup/1.2- to 1.4-L gratin dish, you can make this in a large

(9½-in/24 cm) Pyrex pie plate. An hour in the oven, a few minutes to cool, and nirvana. These go with just about everything, but since they're rich, you'll want to serve them with a hearty green salad, no matter what else.

½ TSP UNSALTED BUTTER

¾ CUP/40 G FRESH BREAD CRUMBS

1 TBSP EXTRA-VIRGIN OLIVE OIL

KOSHER SALT

1½ TSP CHOPPED FRESH ROSEMARY, THYME, OR SAVORY

2 TBSP FINELY GRATED PARMIGIANO-REGGIANO (optional)

¾ CUP/175 ML HEAVY CREAM

½ CUP LOW-SODIUM CHICKEN BROTH

1 TSP DIJON MUSTARD OR PREPARED HORSERADISH (optional)

1 LB/455 G YUKON GOLD POTATOES (about 2 large or 3 medium), peeled; or replace up to 8 oz/225 g of the potato with sweet potato or celery root, peeled

FRESHLY GROUND BLACK PEPPER

1 CUP/110 G GRATED GRUYÈRE, FONTINA, SWISS, OR EMMENTAL (use the large holes on a box grater); or replace up to ½ cup/55 g with ⅛ cup/15 g finely grated Parmigiano-Reggiano or aged Gouda

¼ CUP/35 G FINELY CHOPPED SMOKED HAM, OR 3 TBSP CRUMBLED COOKED BACON (2 slices; optional)

1 *Preheat the oven* to 350°F/175°C (Gas Mark 4). Rub a 5- or 6-cup/1.2- or 1.4-l shallow gratin dish (or a 9½-in/24-cm pie plate) with the butter.

2 *In a small bowl,* combine the bread crumbs with the olive oil, a big pinch of salt, ½ tsp of the chopped herbs, and the Parmigiano (if using). Set aside. In a liquid measure, combine the cream, broth, and mustard (if using), and set aside.

3 *Cut the potatoes* (and sweet potatoes or celery root, if using) in half lengthwise and turn the halves cut side down on a cutting board. With a sharp knife, slice the halves across as thinly as you can (between 1/16 and 1/8 in/1.5 and 3.25 mm is ideal) so that you have thin half-moon pieces. (You can quarter celery root, rather than halve, before slicing.)

4 *Put the potatoes* (and sweet potatoes or celery root, if using) in a mixing bowl. Add ¾ tsp salt, several grinds of black pepper, the cheese, the remaining 1 tsp herbs, the ham (if using), and the cream mixture. Mix well. Using your hands, lift the potatoes out of the bowl and transfer them to the gratin dish, arranging them as evenly as possible. Pour and scrape the liquids and anything remaining in the bowl into the gratin dish and distribute everything evenly, adjusting the potatoes as necessary to get an even top. Using your palms, press down on the potatoes to bring the liquids up and around them as much as possible. (It won't necessarily completely cover them.) Cover the top evenly with the bread crumb mixture.

5 *Bake until the potatoes* are tender when pierced with a fork (check the middle of the dish as well as the sides), the bread crumbs are brown, and the juices around the edges of the gratin have bubbled down and formed a dark brown rim, 55 to 65 minutes. Let cool for about 15 minutes before serving.

Serves 4

Mini-Potato Gratin

On many nights, I've eaten this little gratin for my dinner. Of course, you can make a large gratin (see the foundation recipe on page 194), but I love minis and wanted to include a recipe for an easy classic potato gratin that was just for one or two people. (This serves two as a side dish.) It takes very little time to prepare, but an hour or so to cook and cool. So throw it together (just take care to slice the potato thinly), then go open the mail, feed the dog, and have a glass of wine.

You'll need a mini-gratin dish for this, but they aren't hard to find. Kitchen stores and even discount department stores carry them. Look for one that's a 2-cup/475-ml volume or a little larger (up to 2½ cups/590 ml). Err on the larger size so that the liquids don't bubble over, but don't go too big. Most of the gratin dishes this size are about 8 in/20 cm long and 1¼ to 1½ in/3.25 to 3.75 cm deep. They're usually oval or rectangular. Buy two or more so that you can make individual gratins for friends.

½ CUP/25 G FRESH BREAD CRUMBS

1 TSP EXTRA-VIRGIN OLIVE OIL,
and more for rubbing the dish

1 YUKON GOLD POTATO
(8 oz/225 g), peeled

SCANT ½ TSP KOSHER SALT

FRESHLY GROUND BLACK PEPPER

½ CUP/55 G GRATED GRUYÈRE
(use the large holes on a box grater)

2 TSP FRESH THYME LEAVES

¼ CUP/60 ML HEAVY CREAM

¼ CUP/60 ML PLUS 1 TBSP LOW-SODIUM CHICKEN BROTH

1   *Preheat the oven* to 350°F/175°C (Gas Mark 4). Rub a 2-cup/475-ml shallow gratin dish (about 8 in/20 cm long and 1¼ in/3.25 cm deep) with a little olive oil. In a small bowl, combine the bread crumbs with the 1 tsp olive oil and set aside.

2   *Cut the potato* in half lengthwise and turn both halves cut side down on a cutting board. With a sharp knife, slice the halves across as thinly as you can so that you have thin half-moon pieces. Put the potatoes in a mixing bowl. Add the salt, several grinds of fresh pepper, the Gruyère, thyme leaves, heavy cream, and broth. Mix well. Using your hands, lift the potatoes out of the bowl and transfer them to the gratin dish, arranging them as snugly as possible. Pour and scrape the liquids and any remaining herbs into the gratin dish and distribute them evenly. Press down on the potatoes and adjust them again so that the liquid surrounds them as much as possible. It won't cover the potatoes completely. Cover the top evenly with the bread crumb mixture.

3   *Bake until the potatoes* are tender when pierced with a fork (check the middle of the dish as well as the sides), the bread crumbs are brown, and the juices around the edges of the gratin are quite browned, 50 to 55 minutes. Let cool for 15 to 20 minutes before serving.

Serves 1 or 2

Golden Mushroom and Potato Gratin

Think Christmas Eve and juicy roast beef and you'll know when (and with what) to serve this rich and deeply flavored gratin. Like some of my other potato gratins, this one has the traditional addition of Gruyère, but it's especially at home with golden sautéed mushrooms and a little rosemary.

This gratin takes some time to put together, but I promise, it's worth it, and here's a strategy: Prep and cook the mushrooms before you do anything else, so that they can cool before you mix them with the other ingredients. (You could also cook those a few hours ahead.) You can then slice the potatoes, grate the cheese, and chop the rosemary while the mushrooms cool. Start making this a good 2 hours before you want to serve it, as it takes an hour to cook and benefits from at least 20 minutes of resting time. The gratin does, however, hold well and stays warm for up to 45 minutes, so that could free up some oven space for you.

1½ CUPS/75 G FRESH BREAD CRUMBS	1 TSP MINCED FRESH GARLIC
3 TBSP EXTRA-VIRGIN OLIVE OIL, *and more for the pan*	1¼ LB/570 G YUKON GOLD POTATOES *(about 3 large), peeled*
1½ TSP CHOPPED FRESH ROSEMARY	1½ CUPS/165 G GRATED GRUYÈRE *(use the large holes on a box grater)*
1 LB/455 G CREMINI *(baby bella)* MUSHROOMS, *sliced*	⅔ CUP/160 ML HEAVY CREAM
1½ TSP KOSHER SALT	⅔ CUP/160 ML LOW-SODIUM CHICKEN BROTH

1   *Preheat the oven* to 350°F/175°C (Gas Mark 4). In a small bowl, combine the bread crumbs with 1 Tbsp of the olive oil and ½ tsp of the rosemary. Rub a 2-qt/2-L shallow gratin dish (no more than 2 in/5 cm deep) with a little olive oil.

2   *In a large (12-in/30.5-cm) nonstick skillet,* heat the remaining 2 Tbsp olive oil over medium-high heat. Add the mushrooms and ½ tsp of the salt and cook, stirring occasionally, until the mushrooms are deeply browned, 12 to 14 minutes. Turn the heat down to low, add the garlic, and stir until the garlic is well incorporated and slightly softened, about 1 minute. Remove the pan from the heat. Transfer the mushrooms to a large mixing bowl and let cool for at least 15 minutes while you finish prepping.

3   *Cut each of the potatoes* in half lengthwise and turn both halves cut side down on a cutting board. With a sharp knife, slice the halves across as thinly as you can so that you have thin half-moon pieces. Add the potatoes to the cooled mushrooms. Add the remaining 1 tsp salt and 1 tsp rosemary, the Gruyère, heavy cream, and broth to the bowl. Mix well with a silicone spatula, breaking up the clumps of sliced potatoes and distributing the mushrooms as well as possible. Transfer the whole mixture to the gratin pan, and using your hands, arrange everything so that it's distributed as evenly as possible. Press down with the palms of your hands to let the liquid come around the vegetables (it won't completely cover them). Spread the bread crumb topping evenly over the vegetables.

4   *Bake until the gratin* is quite brown (the edges will be deep brown from the bubbling juices) and the potatoes are tender, 60 to 65 minutes. Pierce the gratin with a fork in several places to see if the potatoes are tender. It should go through all but the centermost potatoes. Let cool for 20 minutes before serving.

Serves 6 to 8

Summer Vegetable and Tomato Tian with Parmesan Bread Crumbs

I first learned to make a tian (a Provençal summer vegetable gratin) in culinary school years ago. Since then I've made so many crowd-pleasing versions of them that they have become a signature Susie dish. For this book, I developed a new version, which I particularly like, because I've marinated the zucchini in a bit of orange juice and balsamic, and added fresh mint. These flavors give this gratin a nice, bright flavor.

I have to tell you my real secret to tian-deliciousness, though: I cook the gratin for a long time—long enough for the juices from the vegetables to greatly reduce and caramelize. (You'll see a dark rim around the inside of the pan where some of the juices have caramelized while bubbling.) With those reduced tomato juices mingling with the sweet browned onions, the flavor is just intense. So don't be tempted to undercook a tian, as even some experienced cooks do. When I say a long time, I only mean an hour or so in most cases, but it's that extra 20 minutes that usually makes the difference.

A tian is fun to put together, because you design it by artfully arranging overlapping rows of vegetables. So pick a pretty gratin dish. I almost always use an oval one, but you can use any baking dish that's shallow and has a 2-qt/475-ml capacity (see Baking Gratins: How It Works, page 192). You will probably wind up with a few extra slices of vegetables after you assemble this, as every gratin comes together a little differently.

Some of my friends who tested this recipe told me they were happy to eat this as a main dish with a salad and some bread. I'm with them, but I often double this and serve it when we're cooking lots of skirt steaks to feed my husband's Argentinian relatives, who never arrive in small numbers.

⅓ CUP/75 ML PLUS 2 TSP EXTRA-VIRGIN OLIVE OIL, *and more for the pan*

1 TBSP FINELY CHOPPED FRESH MINT

1 TBSP FRESH ORANGE JUICE

1 TSP BALSAMIC VINEGAR

KOSHER SALT

12 OZ/340 G ZUCCHINI *(about 2 small)*

1½ LB/680 G SMALL RIPE TOMATOES *(about 5)*

2 MEDIUM ONIONS *(about 10 oz/285 g total), thinly sliced*

½ CUP/25 G FRESH COARSE BREAD CRUMBS

¾ CUP/25 G FINELY GRATED PARMIGIANO-REGGIANO

1 TBSP CHOPPED FRESH PARSLEY

{ Continued }

1   *Preheat the oven* to 375°F/190°C (Gas Mark 5). Grease a shallow 2-qt/2-L gratin dish with a little olive oil.

2   *In a medium mixing bowl,* whisk together the mint, orange juice, balsamic vinegar, 1 Tbsp of the olive oil, and ¼ tsp salt. Slice the zucchini thinly (between ⅛ and ¼ in/ 3.25 and 6.5 mm thick) and slightly on the diagonal. Add them to the bowl and toss well. Core and slice the tomatoes crosswise a little thicker than the zucchini, and arrange them on a large dinner plate or platter. Sprinkle with ¼ tsp salt. Let both the zucchini and the tomatoes sit while you're cooking the onions, or for at least 15 minutes. Toss the zucchini in the marinade occasionally.

3   *Meanwhile,* heat 2 Tbsp of the olive oil in a medium (9- to 10-in/23- to 25-cm) skillet over medium heat. Add the onions and ¼ tsp salt and cook, stirring frequently, until the onions are translucent and start to turn golden brown (they should still have some body), 10 to 12 minutes. Transfer the onions to the gratin dish and spread them out in one layer. Let cool.

4   *In a small bowl,* combine the bread crumbs, 2 tsp of the olive oil, 2 Tbsp of the Parmigiano, the parsley, and a pinch of salt.

5   *Drain the accumulated juices* off the tomatoes and zucchini. Starting at one end of the gratin dish, arrange the vegetables in rows with the slices slightly overlapping each other. (Arrange the first row so the pieces are resting against the back edge of the pan.) I like to alternate between one tomato slice and two zucchini slices (or one if they're very large). Sprinkle a little bit of the Parmigiano over the zucchini slices as you go. If you need to fit in a few more rows, you can compact the rows slightly. Press gently to make sure the vegetables are level. Sprinkle any leftover Parmigiano over the vegetables and drizzle the remaining 2 Tbsp olive oil over them. Sprinkle the bread crumbs on top, letting the vegetables peek out a bit.

6   *Bake until well browned* all over and the juices have bubbled for a while and reduced considerably, 60 to 70 minutes. (The edges of the gratin will be very dark.) Let cool for at least 15 minutes before serving.

Serves 4 to 6

Slow-Roasted Heirloom Tomato Gratin

At the peak of tomato season (mid-September where I live), I start to look for other things to do with big, fat, juicy heirloom tomatoes. Other things, that is, besides eating them raw with a sprinkle of sea salt and a drizzle of olive oil, or eating them in one of my no-cook salads (see page 137). I love to slow-roast tomatoes, because it greatly intensifies their flavor. Usually I roast them (cut in half) on a baking sheet drizzled with lots of olive oil. But it occurred to me that I could also slice them, arrange them in a baking dish, and turn them into a very simple roasted tomato gratin. I tried it for the first time with some yellow Brandywines, and it was delicious. Since then I've even tried it with less-than-spectacular-tomatoes and the long, slow cooking has worked wonders. It only takes 20 minutes or so to prep this, but you'll want to cook it for almost 2 hours. Your home will smell wonderful.

Unlike other gratins in this chapter, there aren't a lot of layers of vegetables here—just overlapping rows of tomatoes. This gives you maximum tomato flavor, with slivers of garlic, fresh thyme leaves, and a little balsamic to enhance it. But don't be surprised at how much the tomatoes shrink in size—this is a flat, thin gratin, but one that's intensely rich in flavor. It also owes its incredibly silky texture to a lot of olive oil (don't be tempted to skimp on this), which permeates the tomatoes as the moisture evaporates. Any oil left in the pan after cooking is delicious on crusty bread. This gratin is really beautiful, so have fun arranging it and trying variously colored tomatoes in it.

3 TBSP PLUS ½ TSP EXTRA-VIRGIN OLIVE OIL	3 TO 4 GARLIC CLOVES, *sliced very thinly crosswise*
2½ LB/1.1 KG LARGE, RIPE HEIRLOOM BEEFSTEAK TOMATOES *(about 3)*	2 TBSP LOOSELY PACKED FRESH THYME LEAVES
¾ TSP KOSHER SALT	½ TSP BALSAMIC VINEGAR
1 TSP SUGAR	

{ Continued }

1   *Preheat the oven* to 350°F/175°C (Gas Mark 4). Rub a 2-qt/2-L shallow baking dish with ½ tsp of the olive oil.

2   *On a cutting board,* preferably a channeled one to catch wandering juices, core the tomatoes. If they're very large (¾ to 1 lb/340 to 455 g), quarter them. If they're on the smaller side, just cut them in half. Turn the quarters and halves cut side down and slice them across into ¼-in-/6.5-mm-thick slices, keeping each group of slices (from the same half or quarter) together as much as possible.

3   *Starting at one end* of the baking dish, arrange one row of overlapping tomato slices across the pan from one side to the other, propping up the slices slightly against the end of the pan. (It's easiest to pick up the slices from a tomato quarter or half and fan them out to make a row.) Season the tomatoes with a tiny bit of the salt and sugar and sprinkle the row with a few slices of the garlic and some of the thyme leaves. Arrange the next row of tomatoes so that they overlap the first quite a bit, and then repeat the seasoning. Continue with rows of overlapping, seasoned tomatoes until you get to the end of the pan. Every so often, you can stop and push the rows back a bit toward the end you started with to compact them somewhat. But don't bunch them up too tightly. Sprinkle any remaining thyme leaves and the balsamic vinegar over all the tomatoes. Drizzle the remaining 3 Tbsp olive oil over all.

4   *Bake until the tomatoes* are very shrunken and the juices in the pan have greatly reduced (they should be barely visible below the edges of the tomatoes), about 1 hour and 45 minutes. The edges of the tomatoes near the center will be slightly browned and those around the sides of the baking dish will be a deep brown. The baking dish itself will be very browned from the spattering and reducing juices. Let cool and eat warm or at room temperature.

Serves 4

{ *Continued* }

Eggplant Parmigiano, Tomato, and Basil Gratin

This isn't really a version of eggplant Parmesan; it's just a very tasty gratin with similar flavors. This is what I would call a tian-style gratin (like the Summer Vegetable and Tomato Tian on page 201), because the slices of vegetables are arranged in overlapping rows from one end of the pan to the other. It looks pretty when served with a green salad, and, of course, eggplant is a natural with lamb. So I would suggest a composed salad. On each dinner plate, arrange a bit of dressed spinach or arugula with a few slices of grilled boneless leg of lamb and a portion of the gratin tucked alongside. To keep the pieces of the gratin together, use a spatula to lift them out of the baking dish.

The only bummer about most baked eggplant dishes (including this one) is that the eggplant needs to be cooked before assembling. Otherwise, it wouldn't cook through in the oven. In this recipe, I roast the eggplant first. I like the flavor of roasted eggplant, and cooking it isn't too fussy. I also think it's a good idea, in this preparation, to score the eggplant skin with a fork before slicing it, as the skin tends to get tough in the oven.

Once you've begun to assemble the gratin, if you find that you have too many vege-tables or are coming up short, you can compact or expand the rows slightly as you go.

1 LB/455 G GLOBE EGGPLANT (*about 1 medium-large*)

SCANT ½ CUP/120 ML EXTRA-VIRGIN OLIVE OIL

KOSHER SALT

2 MEDIUM ONIONS (*about 10 oz/285 g total*), *thinly sliced*

1 LB/455 G SMALL TOMATOES (*about 3*)

4 TBSP CHOPPED FRESH BASIL

⅔ CUP/20 G FINELY GRATED PARMIGIANO-REGGIANO

½ CUP/25 G FRESH BREAD CRUMBS

2 TSP PREPARED BLACK OLIVE TAPENADE

1   *Preheat the oven* to 450°F/230°C (Gas Mark 8). Line a heavy-duty sheet pan with a piece of parchment paper.

2   *Trim the ends* of the eggplant. Score the eggplant skin by dragging a fork down it lengthwise. Repeat the scoring over the whole eggplant. Cut the eggplant in half lengthwise; cut each half crosswise into ½-in-/1.25-cm-thick half-moon slices. Using a pastry brush, coat the parchment paper with 2 tsp of the olive oil and arrange the eggplant slices in one layer on the sheet pan. Brush the tops of the eggplant slices with 2 Tbsp of the olive oil and season with ¼ tsp salt. Roast until the eggplant is tender and lightly browned, 20 to 25 minutes. (The undersides will be slightly browner, and the slices will be somewhat shrunken.) Reduce the oven temperature to 375°F/190°C (Gas Mark 5). Set the eggplant aside while you prepare the rest of the ingredients.

3   *Grease a shallow* 2-qt/2-L gratin dish with a little of the olive oil.

4   *In a medium (9- to 10-in/23- to 25-cm) skillet* over medium heat, heat 2 Tbsp of the olive oil. Add the onions and ¼ tsp salt and cook, stirring frequently, until the onions are a light golden brown but still have some body, 10 to 12 minutes. Transfer the onions to the gratin dish and spread them out in one layer. Let cool.

5   *Core the tomatoes* and slice them lengthwise (through the stem). Put each tomato half, cut side down, on the cutting board, and cut each half crosswise into ¼-in-/6.5-mm-thick slices. Put the tomato slices on a shallow plate and let them shed a bit of their juice.

6   *In a small bowl*, combine 2 Tbsp of the basil with the Parmigiano. In another small bowl, combine the bread crumbs with 2 tsp olive oil, a pinch of salt, and 2 Tbsp of the basil-Parmigiano mixture.

7   *Spread the tapenade* over the onions in the gratin dish. Sprinkle the remaining 2 Tbsp basil over all. Starting at one end of the gratin dish, arrange the eggplant and tomatoes (prop the first row up a bit against the edge of the dish) in rows with the slices slightly overlapping each other. Alternate between one tomato slice and one eggplant slice, sprinkling a little bit of the basil-Parmigiano mixture over each slice as you go.

8   *Season the gratin* with ¼ tsp salt and drizzle 2 Tbsp of the olive oil over the vegetables. If you have any leftover basil-Parmigiano, sprinkle it over the vegetables and then cover with the bread crumb mixture, letting the vegetables peek out a bit.

9   *Bake until well browned* all over and the juices have bubbled for a while and reduced considerably, 60 to 70 minutes. (The edges of the gratin will be very dark.) Let cool for at least 15 minutes before serving.

Serves 6

Christmas Kale Gratin with Sun-Dried Tomatoes

Winter is slow to come on Martha's Vineyard. Because the island is surrounded by warm water, the weather stays mild in the fall. We're still harvesting corn and tomatoes in late October, and hardy winter greens like kale keep right on growing through December. When I put together this lightly creamy gratin, the red in the sun-dried tomatoes and the green in the kale made me think of Christmas, though I'd be just as happy to eat it on New Year's Day with a good baked ham. No matter when you serve it, it's a good way to get smaller people to eat their greens.

I find that the cream and cheese in this gratin mellow the earthy flavor of kale, and with the help of sun-dried tomatoes, they give this dish a very pleasing flavor. You could substitute an equal amount (about 8 oz/225 g raw) of cooked spinach, chard, Russian kale, Tuscan kale, or mustard greens in this, but if you use the mustard greens, keep in mind that they will retain their spicy flavor (see page 116 for boiling times). Boiling and draining the greens is the only fussy thing here; the rest of this gratin is simple to put together. It's the quickest-cooking gratin in the chapter; it only needs 20 to 25 minutes in the oven.

½ TSP UNSALTED BUTTER

1 CUP/50 G FRESH BREAD CRUMBS

3 TBSP FINELY GRATED PARMIGIANO-REGGIANO

1 TBSP EXTRA-VIRGIN OLIVE OIL

KOSHER SALT

1 BUNCH KALE *(14 to 15 oz/400 g to 425 g)*, *stemmed, leaves ripped into 2-in/5-cm pieces (yielding 7 to 8 oz/200 to 225 g)*

1 CUP/240 ML HEAVY CREAM

FRESHLY GROUND BLACK PEPPER

2 TBSP CHOPPED DRAINED OIL-PACKED SUN-DRIED TOMATOES

1 CUP/110 G GRATED GRUYÈRE OR SWISS CHEESE *(use the large holes of a box grater)*

1   *Preheat the oven* to 400°F/205°C (Gas Mark 6). Rub a 5- or 6-cup/1.2- or 1.4-L shallow gratin dish (or a 9½-inch/24-cm pie plate) with the butter. In a small bowl, combine the bread crumbs, Parmigiano, olive oil, and a pinch of salt.

2   *Fill a wide 4- to 5-qt/3.8- to 4.7-L Dutch-oven* three-quarters full with water, add 2 tsp salt, and bring to a boil. Add the kale to the boiling water and start timing immediately. Taste a leaf after 5 minutes. It should not be tough or rubbery. If it is, cook for 1 to 2 minutes more. Drain the kale in a colander in the sink and run cool water over it just until it's cool enough to handle. Press down on the kale to remove as much water as possible. Transfer the kale to a mixing bowl by the handful, squeezing each handful again to remove additional water.

3   *In a small saucepan* over medium heat, bring the cream to a boil, watching it carefully. As soon as it boils (don't let it boil over), turn the heat down and simmer until it reduces by one-quarter, about 5 minutes (watch carefully; you should have ¾ cup/175 ml). Remove the cream from the heat and season it with ¼ tsp salt and a few grinds of pepper.

4   *Add the sun-dried tomatoes* and the cheese to the bowl of kale. Loosely toss everything together. (The mixture doesn't have to be too thoroughly combined; just be sure to break up any big clumps of cheese.) Spread out the mixture evenly in the gratin dish. Pour the cream over all. Cover the gratin with the bread crumb mixture, spreading it out as evenly as possible.

5   *Bake the gratin* until the crumbs are well browned and the cream has reduced to below the top of the gratin, 20 to 25 minutes.

Serves 4 to 5

Harvest Gratin of Butternut Squash, Corn, and Leeks

This lovely collection of late-summer, early-fall flavors is one of my favorites—a definite farmers' market special. Sautéed leeks mingle with fresh corn kernels, garlic, thyme, lemon, and Parmigiano (and a little cream) to give butternut squash a big boost. The squash is cut into small dice so that it mixes evenly with the corn and leeks, and so that it cooks through in the gratin. If you buy peeled squash, the prep does not take long.

If you like, you can add a little bit of diced smoked ham or cooked bacon to the mix. While the gratin goes with a lot of things, it begs for crab cakes or even fish cakes.

The squash will absorb most of the cream-broth mixture as it cooks, and as those liquids reduce, they will leave quite a bit of browning around the edges of the pan. When the gratin is done, bubbles from the liquid will be barely detectable around the edges. But you can also check for doneness by poking the squash with a fork or knife.

1 TBSP PLUS ½ TSP UNSALTED BUTTER

1 CUP/50 G FRESH BREAD CRUMBS

1 TBSP EXTRA-VIRGIN OLIVE OIL

KOSHER SALT

1 MEDIUM LEEK (*about 2½ oz/70 g; white and light green parts*), *diced and washed*

1½ TSP MINCED FRESH GARLIC

1⅓ CUPS (*about 7oz/200 g*) FRESH CORN KERNELS (*from 2 large ears; for cutting tips see page 67*)

FRESHLY GROUND BLACK PEPPER

⅓ CUP/80 ML HEAVY CREAM

⅓ CUP/80 ML LOW-SODIUM CHICKEN BROTH

½ TSP FINELY GRATED LEMON ZEST

1 TSP FINELY CHOPPED FRESH THYME

12 OZ/340 G PEELED AND SEEDED BUTTERNUT SQUASH, *cut into ½-inch/1.25-cm dice (about 2½ cups)*

⅓ CUP/10 G FINELY GRATED PARMIGIANO-REGGIANO

1. *Preheat the oven* to 400°F/205°C/ (Gas Mark 6). Rub a 5- or 6-cup/1.2- or 1.4-L shallow gratin dish (or a 9½-inch/24-cm pie plate) with ½ tsp of the butter.

2. *In a small bowl,* combine the bread crumbs, olive oil, and a pinch of salt and mix well.

3. *In a medium (9- to 10-in/23- to 25-cm) nonstick skillet,* melt the remaining 1 Tbsp butter over medium-low heat. Add the leek and a pinch of salt, and cook, stirring, until softened and just starting to turn golden, about 5 minutes. Add the garlic and stir well to incorporate it. Add the corn kernels, ¼ tsp salt, and a few grinds of black pepper. Cook, stirring, until the corn has lost its raw look, is glistening, and is slightly shrunken, 2 to 3 minutes. Remove the pan from the heat and let the mixture cool for a couple of minutes.

4   *Combine the heavy cream* and the broth in a liquid measure. Add the lemon zest, thyme, ½ tsp salt, and a few grinds of pepper. Stir to mix well and set aside.

5   *Add the squash* to the corn-leek mixture and toss to loosely combine. Transfer the mixture to the gratin dish and arrange as evenly as possible. Sprinkle the Parmigiano over the vegetables. Pour the cream mixture over everything, distributing the herbs and lemon as well as possible (you can stir them gently in the pan to distribute better). Be sure to scrape out any seasonings left in the liquid measure. Sprinkle the bread crumb mixture evenly over all.

6   *Bake until the crumb topping* is deep golden and the squash is tender when pierced with a fork, 40 to 45 minutes. The juices should have bubbled below the surface of the vegetables, leaving browned bits in a line around the edges of the pan.

Serves 4 to 5

Acknowledgments of Kindness, Grace, Time, and Patience

If you think you might someday like to write a cookbook, I advise you to be really kind and considerate to everyone you know, as you will need them to help you, in a big way. I can hardly think of a person (or animal!) I know who hasn't helped me with this book, my first. (And guess what, guys, I hope not the last. This was fun, don't you think so?!)

I borrowed friends' kitchens, stole their dishes and tablecloths, cooked on their grills. I took vegetables out of their gardens and spices out of their spice racks. I asked every professional cook I know for advice and opinions. I made my mother and sister keep testing recipes, even after everyone else had smiled and said, We're done, right?

Best of all, I subjected four huge hogs—Sally, Harley, Penny, and Jelly Bean—to frequent taste tests. They wanted me to tell you that they're really partial to the potato gratins. But, in a pinch, they will eat fennel fronds, Swiss chard stems, and whole acorn squash. Or anything else

Seriously, I now have to begin the parade of names, but it pains me to have to reduce them to not much more than a list (or you will stop reading this if you haven't already). Just to be fair, I'm going to start with those who came in at the beginning.

To everyone listed here, all my gratitude and love.

To my literary agent, Sarah Jane Freymann, for alighting gracefully on the idea (and the title) for this book, and for unconditionally supporting me every step of the way. She is a very special lady. And to Pam Anderson, cook and human being extraordinaire, for generously loaning me Sarah Jane.

To Bill LeBlond, the cookbook editor of every girl's dreams. If I could have genie-d him up to accept my proposal I would have. When he did, I leapt for joy. And to Doug Ogan, Anne Donnard, Ben Kasman, Peter Perez, and David Hawk, my unseen supporters at Chronicle who backed him up, I am indebted to you.

To a world of very fine folks at the Taunton Press, my home for eleven years. And especially to my staff at *Fine Cooking* magazine, who so graciously let me go off to be a writer even when they knew that meant they were stuck with the issue plans: Jennifer Armentrout, Rebecca Freedman, Laura Giannatempo, Lisa Waddle, Denise Mickelsen, Annie Giammattei, Pam Winn, Enid Johnson, Kim Landi, Allison Ehri Kreitler, Dabney Gough, Sarah Breckenridge, Sharon

Anderson, and Kelly Gearity. Not only did they let me go, but they let me keep writing for them. My special thanks to Sarah for putting up with my long blogs, to Rebecca and Laura for putting up with my long features, to Jennifer for putting up with my long-winded questions about everything, and to *Fine Cooking*'s new editor, Laurie Buckle, for putting up with me altogether! Thanks also to Jennifer, Sarah, and Denise for testing recipes. And to Annie for Annie. And to Karen Lutjen for all those laughs. And to Maria Taylor, my boss and my friend, for her support and understanding. Lastly, to my fellow chief editors and friends, Jeff Kolle and Kevin Ireton, who waited patiently with me to hear the words, "Your book is sold." You're next, boys.

To the five women who constituted Team Susie in a year I will never forget: Abby Adis, Janet Bertoldi, Mary Hulbert, Gail Wiggin, and Heather MacLeod.

To Jessica Bard, the most fun and fabulous cook/friend a girl can have, who tested every single one of these recipes not just with professionalism, but also with enthusiasm and excitement. I simply could not have done this book without her, nor would it have been half as much fun. Jessica, there just aren't enough thank-yous in the world for you.

To Tony Rosenfeld, a more thoughtful and supportive friend there could not be. Thanks not just for your help with the book, but for that keeping-in-touch thing you do.

To Ali Berlow, an angel who appeared to me not long after I arrived on Martha's Vineyard. (Thank you, John Abrams!) She lent me her kitchen, her friendship, her music, her meat loaf, her wisdom, and even her husband. (Okay, just as a taste tester. Thanks, Sam.). Ali, thanks for living this book with me. I treasure that.

To all of my new farmer and foodie friends on the Vineyard who made me feel so comfortable so quickly: Randi Baird, Noli Taylor, Heidi Feldman, and, most especially, Liz Thompson—and Jeffry, Oscar, Lucy, and all the animals. And to Chris Fischer—I wish I hadn't eaten that pig, but I'm not sorry I got to travel those back roads with you. Thanks for showing me around. And to Jim and Debbie Athearn and Morning Glory Farm—what an inspiration.

To Jeff Young, for Tamarack Lane, and everything else. To Roy Riley, for the ultimate in patience and for lending a hand. (The first copy is yours.) And to every one of you who answered my e-mails and said, "Yes, I'll test a recipe!" Cathy Cavender, Kimberly Masibay, Florence Scheffer, Lucy Irwin, Chuck Schoendorf, Lin De Young, Margaret Steele, Janet Bertoldi, and Steve Hunter. My aunt, Randi Evans. My cousin, Kari Evans. My sister, Eleanor Evans. My mother, Pauletta Evans. My best friend, Eliza Peter.

And to Eliza, for more than just recipe testing—for everything, forty-seven years and counting. And to the third diamond in our crown, Liz Gray, for every twenty-four hours.

To Steve Hunter, for your friendship and your ridiculous sense of humor, and for all those props you lent me for the photo shoot—including your beautiful ceramics.

ACKNOWLEDGMENTS OF KINDNESS, GRACE, TIME, AND PATIENCE

To Ben Fink, for all our photo shoots together, but mostly for making me feel so good about this one. You know how happy I am! To Michelli Knauer, for your spirit, your beautiful food styling, your company, and your doggie aplomb. And to Safaya Tork, for all your help and your eggplant, too. And to Vanessa Dina at Chronicle, for your design inspiration and support during the photo shoot and to Jessica Hische for the design of this book.

To Katie Hutchison, for the glam shots, and to Chris Hufstader, for the Chris-and-Katie check-ins.

To Li Agen, for your amazing thoroughness and for your willingness to hang in with me there at the end, copyediting a boat load of recipes in record time. Promise me you'll never say no!

To Deborah Kops, for your incredibly graceful editing of one bulky manuscript, and to Sarah Billingsley, for making me feel welcome at Chronicle and for your sensitive shepherding and shaping of my book.

To Martha Holmberg, for getting this whole ridiculous thing started. You are still my inspiration, girl, and I love you.

To Sarah Jay, for Life 101, and a few hundred deadlines that made all this seem like a cakewalk.

To chefs George Germon, Johanne Killeen, and Katherine Alford, for setting me on the right path. And to chef Lenny Green, wherever you are, for your integrity and for not killing me on my first day of work.

To the gals in Rowayton, Lynn Anderson, Joan Dereght, Karen Wolfskehl, and Ann Eydt, for moral support and good laughs. And to Lynn, for letting us bust your iron at the photo shoot.

To my dad and mom, Bob and Pauletta Evans, and my sister, Eleanor Evans, with lots of love—what an amazing family of cooks (and eaters!) to call my own. Thanks for showing me the way and putting up with my finicky taste buds all those years. And a big thanks for putting up with the grown-up me, especially these last couple of years.

To Algy, for your patience with photo shoots, my deadlines, and those all-vegetable dinners. You are my idea of amazing grace. And to Cath Middleton, Anna Middleton, Anne Petersen, and Mary Claire Petersen, for your photo-shoot patience, love, and support.

And to George, for a million tastings (good grub!) and a million moments of patience, love, and understanding. Not to mention doggie day care. Gus and Scout, we love you. Sweet doggie dreams forever.

—*Susie*

Index

INDEX